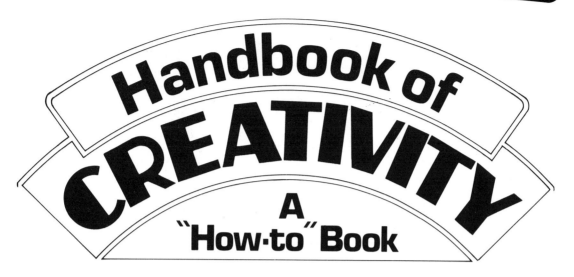

Handbook of CREATIVITY
A "How-to" Book

by

Judy Dorsett

STANDARD PUBLISHING
Cincinnati, Ohio   3226

Library of Congress Cataloging in Publication Data
Dorsett, Judy.
  Handbook of creativity.

    1. Christian education—Teaching methods. 2. Christian education of children. 3. Activity
programs in Christian education. I. Title.
BV1534.D66 1984   268'.432   84-8668
ISBN 0-87239-729-7

CONTENTS

I hear 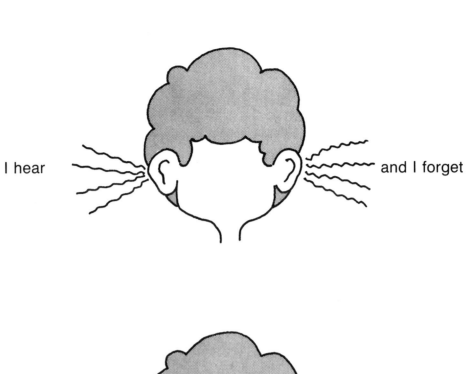 and I forget

I see and I remember

I DO  and I UNDERSTAND

What IS Creativity?

"I'm just *not* creative!" Have you ever heard someone say those words in frustration? Have you ever said them about yourself?

Many of us have allowed ourselves to be caught in the trap of thinking negatively about our creative ability and potential. We have lost that delightful quality of childhood—the joy of discovery.

As Christians we desire to continue growing into a likeness of Christ. Occasionally we stub our toes, fall down, or fail entirely. Then God, who loves us like a father, helps us up and renews our courage for another try. The same thing happens with our development of new skills and talents.

If someone asked you to name the most creative being known, what would you answer? Most of us would say without hesitation, "God, of course!"

In whose image were *we* created? We are told in Genesis 5:1, 2, "In the day that God created man, in the *likeness of God* made he him; male and female created he them, and blessed them." Therefore, we are like the most creative being known. But somehow, as individuals, we have lost sight of the creative capacity built into us by God himself. We may see only the creativity of others and measure ourselves against their talents. In our secret hearts we think, "I could never do that."

Imagine Michelangelo when he first began sculpturing. Was his first attempt a masterpiece? Perhaps his second? We will never know. He must have been talented to attract notice. However, some of his best known works were completed when he was seventy-five and eighty.

Thomas Edison, the famous creator of the electric light bulb and many other things, had only three months of formal education. But he had an inquiring mind and a desire to try. He defined genius as "one percent inspiration and ninety-nine percent perspiration."

Few of us will ever be Michelangelos or Edisons. However, as Christians working with children, we are sculptors and light-givers. The minds and hearts of those we teach are moldable material. As teachers we have the opportunity and joy of being God's channel of light and understanding.

God's creation is full of infinite variety. His knowledge and ability are immeasurable. We are told in the book of John that Jesus—the Word—actively participated in creation. In 1 Corinthians 2:16 God's Word states, "We have the mind of Christ." When we become Christians, we understand spiritual matters more fully. We also have available an unlimited source of knowledge about natural talents, gifts, and creative abilities—the mind of Christ.

How will we discover our personal bit of that creative ability, that special gift, or that natural talent if we do not explore?

In our exploration, should we give up if there are failures? No. Should we try something different if our attempts in one area do not meet with success? Certainly. Should we compare our talent or gift, whether large or small in our own eyes, with anyone else's? Certainly not. Unfortunately negative comparisons are a common human failing.

God reminds us in His Word that as members of the spiritual body we are all equally important though our spiritual gifts differ. It is the same with our natural gifts and talents.

Joy and satisfaction come from discovering our own abilities. When those abilities enable us to share God's love and reach others more effectively for Him, we find fulfillment.

We may begin with timid steps and little confidence. We may begin at eighteen, thirty-eight, or fifty-eight. But if we keep our hand in our Father's and our eyes on Him rather than on others, our steps become stronger and our abilities increase.

(Some of the border sketches from this book—such as this one—are used in the text itself as dividers. This has been done to show how many ways the borders provided can be used.)

The following True-False Quiz may help clarify ideas about creativity and ability. Many of us have misconceptions regarding what it means to be creative. *(Answers are on the following pages.)*

True—False Quiz

1. ____ People are either creative or they are not.
2. ____ Creative people are talented in everything they do.
3. ____ Preparation has little to do with creativity.
4. ____ Prayer has no effect on creative ability.
5. ____ Creative ideas come in mysterious flashes.
6. ____ Creative people feel comfortable with a mess.
7. ____ Children are more creative than adults.
8. ____ Special training is necessary to be creative.
9. ____ To be creative means to have brand-new ideas.

6

10. ____ Using someone else's idea is plagiarizing.
11. ____ Creative people try to learn from their failures.
12. ____ People may think my ideas are stupid.
13. ____ Creative ability can be discovered at any age.
14. ____ I am creative.

True—False Quiz Answers

1. False. Everyone has creative potential. There are few individuals who have no natural talent or ability. Many people consider a talent or a gift worthwhile only if it falls into the category of "art." The teacher with a warm, outgoing personality who reaches out and makes each child feel especially welcome has a gift. Taking time to listen is a talent. Many have gifts or talents in their lives but do not consider them or perhaps even recognize them. A teacher does not have to be gifted in every area to include those areas in his or her teaching. For example, there are many ways to include music even though the teacher isn't musical. Someone who enjoys arts and crafts could work on a part-time basis if the regular teacher doesn't feel confident with art projects. Being a creative teacher may mean doing what you do well. So be a creative manager and bring in people who excel in the areas in which you do not.

2. False. Each person has his or her own areas of expertise. However, those who are willing to try new things often find they have abilities previously unrecognized. They may appear more talented, but in fact have only been more willing to experiment.

    Although the parable Jesus taught in Matthew 25:14-30 concerned stewardship of money, the story idea and use of the word "talent" are applicable to this question. The servant given five talents went out and developed five more. The servant given two talents increased those two to four. But the servant given one talent was so fearful he hid his talent. The master considered him a slothful fellow and took his one talent from him. The analogy for us—develop our talents and abilities, build on what we have. If we are so fearful that we hide and doubt the talent we've been given, we will lose it.

3. False. Preparation has a great deal to do with creativity. It is a very rare person who can pick up the Sunday-school lesson manual ten minutes before class and be creative. It takes time to prepare special activities. A teacher must be familiar with the lesson idea to receive innovative thoughts about presenting it. Additional information about lesson preparation will be presented later.

4. False. Prayer and preparation are partners in creativity. When the quar-

terly theme and specific lesson truth are in mind before the lesson; when those ideas are taken before the Lord in meditative, conversational prayer; and when the mind is willing and open to His inspiration—new thoughts develop.

5. True or False. Even when one has prayed and thought, it is sometimes surprising how the Lord answers. True, the thoughts seem to come mysteriously. False, the creative inspiration isn't really mysterious because we know it comes from God.

6. Generally true. It is OK to make a mess. Those who enjoy cooking, sewing, gardening, home renovating, machine repairing, or any of a number of arts know the creative process is sometimes very messy. Projects may even set out for a few days or weeks as they develop. A mess can be tidied when the project is completed.

7. False. Adults have often closed their minds to the possibility of developing new talents or gifts. Previous disappointments or failures may have led them to believe they are not talented. Children are still exploring their world and discovering things about themselves. They often appear more creative because they are still willing to try and are not overly critical of their first or second attempts.

8. False. It is not necessary to have a teaching degree or musical or art training. It helps, of course. All that is truly necessary is a love for those you teach, an inquiring mind, and a willingness to try.

9. False. Creativity seldom means doing something "brand-new." There are many forms of creativity. Creativity may be simply recognizing the adaptability of a well-known game, puzzle, or idea to the needs of your group. Many of the ideas in this book are adaptations of ordinary, everyday games, things, and ideas.

10. Generally false. Ideas usually belong in the common domain. Each person may use an idea differently. To take another's exact and specific use of an idea, to photocopy in avoidance of purchase, or to claim someone's product or presentation as your own would be plagiarizing. Taking an idea, adapting it to fit your own need and making your own materials is acceptable. If there are doubts, write to the company, discuss what you wish to do, and ask permission in case that is necessary.

11. True. Failure of an idea doesn't mean the idea was poor. It may have been either too complicated or too easy for the age group with whom you work. It may have been used with the wrong combination of children. Personality or discipline problems can sabotage a project which essentially was good. Analyze what happened. See if the problem can

be corrected. Save the idea for use with another age or group. Don't give up.

12. Generally false. Most people lack the courage to try something new if it means doing that new thing in front of other people. But others usually admire ingenuity. They may even envy those with the confidence to attempt something new. Talk with friends you consider creative. You will find, whatever their age or ability, they felt insecure in their first steps of discovery. The most experienced and talented feel hesitant and uncertain at times.

13. True. Remember Grandma Moses. One of the delights of living is knowing there are many new experiences and discoveries if we reach out for them.

14. True. Really! You were created in God's image. You have the mind of Christ. You have gifts and talents. You have creative potential. Don't try to fit into anyone else's mold. Be yourself. Be willing to try. God bless you!

The following story from the *Royal Ranger Pioneer Handbook* is used by permission of the Gospel Publishing House. It tells about finding our real potential.

"I guess everyone knows the stories of Rudolph the Red-Nosed Reindeer and the Ugly Duckling. Both of them were downhearted, thinking they were not much good, when actually their times had not arrived.

"Some of our greatest athletes were weaklings as boys. Some of our greatest inventors were considered stupid by their teachers, and some of our greatest political leaders were failures in their early lives. I recall a story about an eagle that had been taken from its nest by a farmer when it was young. He had clipped one wing so it could not fly away, and he had put it with the young chickens. The eagle soon felt right at home with the chickens, ate chicken feed, and seemed almost like a chicken.

"One day a visitor stopped at the farm and chanced to see the young eagle with the chickens.

"'Hey, where did you get that eagle,' he asked. 'What's it doing with the chickens?'

"'Well,' the farmer replied, 'maybe he was an eagle once, but he's a chicken now. He's been living with them so long he even looks like a chicken. Even though his wing has regrown, he'll never fly again.'

"'That's were you are wrong, my friend,' said the visitor. 'Once an eagle, always an eagle. I can get him to fly.'

"The farmer agreed to let him try, so the visitor caught the eagle. He held the eagle in his hands and talked to it. 'You are an eagle. You belong to the sky.' Tossing it as high in the air as he could, he shouted, 'Now, fly!' But the eagle floated down to earth and ate food again with the chickens.

"This was a challenge to the visitor, so the next morning he put the eagle in a sack and carried it up a mountain. He was determined to toss the eagle from the highest point of the cliff, if necessary, to make him fly. When taken from the sack, the eagle felt the wind of the mountain heights, caught the brightness of the sun, and saw itself high above the valley. It struggled free from the visitor's hands, spread its wings, and went off the cliff. Now the eagle knew it was an eagle. Although it lost height at first, it started to circle and gradually rose higher and higher into the sky. It never again returned to the farmer's yard to live with the chickens."

We are really eagles in disguise. God created us to fly, but we've lived with the chickens. We need to shake off feelings of inadequacy and discover who we really are.

1 Corinthians 13:1-13
A Paraphrase for Teachers

Though I speak in the many languages of men, and with the eloquence of angels, and have not love, I am become as clanging pans, or a tinkling wind chime.

And though I have the gift of creative genius, and understand all teaching techniques, and all art processes; and though I have such charisma, so that I could entrance millions, and have not love, I am nothing.

And though I give all my goods for programs and supplies, and though I give every moment of my life, and have not love, it profiteth me nothing.

Love is tremendously patient, and kind; love does not envy the gifts of others, love does not consider its talent superior, is not prideful.

Doth not behave itself ungraciously, seeketh not her own way, is not easily angered, thinketh no evil toward students or fellow workers;

Rejoiceth not in the mistakes of others, but rejoiceth in their success and encourageth them;

Beareth with others, believeth in their abilities, hopeth for all things to prosper for them, endureth with them as they grow.

Love never faileth; but whether there be genius, it shall fail; whether there be persuasive speakers, they shall cease; whether there be human knowledge, it shall vanish away.

For we know in part, are fearful and doubt ourselves.

But when we open our thoughts to God, He fills our minds with courage and ideas.

When I was younger, I spoke hesitantly, my understanding was less complete, I thought myself unable; but as I matured, I put away immature behaviour and beliefs.

For now we are still growing, but God shall bring us into His likeness, capable, creative, and mature.

And now abideth technique, talent, love, these three, but the greatest of these is love.

Preparation — Pain or Pleasure?

It takes more time to be unorganized than to be organized.

Most people would disagree with that statement. However, if you were to ask people who have tried both ways, most will tell you it takes more nervous energy, worry, and hassle to be unorganized than to be organized.

Being organized means giving yourself time to plan ahead. It means knowing what your lesson is about *before* Sunday morning. It means thinking about the children in your department. What do they need to learn at this stage in their lives? Do any of them have special needs or home problems? God has answers for all our needs, and we must help children see that those answers come from His Word. How can they if we hurry through a poorly planned, poorly executed lesson?

There are many ways to organize ideas and materials for lessons. The following ideas work for those who use them. They don't take too long to implement, and they aren't too much for any person in the department if each works on one special thing a quarter.

If materials, games, bulletin boards, examples of art projects, and puzzle masters are kept for future use, the teachers soon have varied and permanent supplies. This cuts down greatly the amount of time needed to be spent when those lessons or topics arrive again.

Materials may be stored in labeled manila folders or folders made of butcher paper. These folders may be kept in separate divisions for games, puzzles, art, lessons, bulletin board ideas, etc. Most publishing companies repeat their lesson series every year or two. Folders could be arranged and stored according to quarters. That way all materials used for a particular quarter would be available when the series is repeated. Another way to store materials is by subject—Lessons about David, Lessons about Jesus, etc. Any system is better than *no* system. Folders may be stored in a drawer in the class area. Cardboard boxes make a good drawer substitute if only shelves are available. When placing folders in drawers or boxes, be certain to stand them on their side. Folders stored one on top of the other in a box or drawer tend to get buried or allow items to slip out.

At the end of this section are sample worksheets. The first one is for identifying the quarterly lesson theme, analyzing lesson type, and for noting memory verses, appropriate songs, special bulletin boards, or craft projects. Teachers' lesson manuals are usually given out a week or two in advance of the new quarter. This sheet works best for the teacher if he or she fills it in before the quarter begins or during the first week. When this sheet is completed, the teacher can see at a glance if too many lessons in a row follow the same type and if there are adequate games or crafts.

Being able to spot weaknesses in the overall plan for the quarter helps the teacher see where he or she can vary the lesson type or presentation, change the game or craft to better suit the group, or add a game or puzzle to a lesson that may not be long enough to fill the allowed time. If there are obvious open spots in the quarterly overview sheet, jot down ideas on the sheet for the weak areas. The teacher will have between one and three months to prepare these special fill-in projects, depending on where in the quarter's sequence the lesson being adjusted falls. When this sheet is completed, hang it in a conspicuous place such as the inside of the cupboard door for drinking glasses. Both men and women use this door often. The sheet will be a reminder to prepare for lessons coming up and will keep reminding the teacher of special projects for which he or she must plan. It will keep lesson truths in mind so the Lord can give those inspired thoughts of new or different ways to handle the lessons.

The purpose of the second worksheet is to help the total Sunday-school department plan for the quarter. It only takes one staff meeting of an hour or so at the beginning of the quarter to work out assignments. Each person provides input. Plans for the quarter may be changed when the need arises, but basically everyone knows when and for what he or she is responsible. When the assignment sheet is completed, hang it on the same cupboard door with the quarterly overview sheet.

If you teach in a department with several grades that has a general opening together, certain people may always perform the same jobs so a planning sheet for quarterly assignments may not be as necessary. Each teacher may always teach to his or her own group. Interaction between teachers for preparing games or puzzles is more limited because each teacher has been independent in his or her presentation. Even in this more standard Sunday-school situation special project preparation, puzzle development, games or crafts appropriate to that grade or division level may be shared among teachers. If the teachers rotate the making or planning of these special projects, all benefit and none are unfairly overworked.

If the department is only one grade level, more freedom is possible in structuring the Sunday-school hour. The assignment sheet is most helpful then. Most of the children will be on or near that grade level so it won't be as difficult to plan something within the ability range of the children. Also, teaching is easier if the lesson can be taught to the entire group. The teachers may rotate Sundays they teach, and so have two or three Sundays in which to prepare a really special lesson. Other activities in the department may also be rotated, so each person has something different to do each Sunday, and everyone gets a chance to try the various aspects of teaching. This permits teachers to devote all their planning time during the week to *one* activity rather than several. In this way, teachers develop skills in many areas and have time to prepare. They grow and benefit and the children learn and enjoy.

(Permission is given to photocopy the worksheets.)

QUARTERLY OVERVIEW SHEET

Quarterly Theme

DATE	LESSON TITLE	LESSON TYPE	MUSIC	MEMORY VERSE	CRAFT/GAME	BULLETIN BOARD SPECIAL EVENTS

QUARTERLY ASSIGNMENT SHEET

Date	Presession	Opening	Music	Lesson	Game	Art	Special Activity

Vary Lesson Type or Presentation

Lessons in most Sunday-school curriculum follow a lecture-type lesson. Many include questions for and conversations with children. Most include some pictures and a flannelgraph lesson or two. Occasionally, the teacher's resource packet will include a game or craft-type activity. Since the quarter usually has thirteen Sundays, there is often not enough variation in lesson type or presentation.

The following sections in this book provide many ideas and instructions for varying your lesson type or presentation, art and craft projects, puzzles, games as reviews of curriculum or Bible verses, and other activities supportive of the Sunday-school lesson. A brief overview on how to add variety and maintain student interest in the lesson is given here.

Films, Filmstrips

Check with your superintendent or department supervisor. Some churches have a supply of filmstrips with cassette, record, or paper scripts. Many churches have a central library of films and filmstrips available for teacher use. Many churches have such a lending library on a regional level. Your superintendent should be able to help you find out what's available.

If you make an overview sheet of upcoming lessons before the quarter begins, a department superintendent or teacher can order an appropriate filmstrip for one or two lessons. Plan, if possible, to show these as a break in a series of too many lecture-type lessons.

If the filmstrip or film does not cover exactly what your lesson discusses, but covers most of the basic information, add to what the film gives with a short discussion before or after it.

Flannelgraph or Magnetic Pictures

If the teacher's resource packet includes flannelgraph pictures to accompany lessons, use them. If you feel unsure about your ability to do so, practice at home several times. Cut or punch out the pictures and place them in the order in which they will be presented during the story. This helps prevent confusion when in front of your students. If you feel insecure about presenting a flannelgraph lesson, ask someone with experience to teach you, and observe their technique.

Magnetic pictures are paper pictures which are cut out, have small pieces of magnetic tape attached, and are placed on a paper background which rests in a metal holder. These usually come in the teacher's resource packet. They are used in the same way flannelgraph pictures are used.

Food

It is possible to include a small snack or treat as added emphasis for the Sunday-school lesson when food is part of the story or theme.

Adding food does not change the basic lesson type. It makes an interesting break in the presentation, and it makes the lesson *seem* different to the children.

See the section on food for something edible as part of the story.

Research

This technique can be used with older children to help them teach each other. Various aspects of the lesson can be assigned to different small groups. Information needed for a lesson could be related to modes of travel, food eaten and how it was grown, type of clothing worn, jobs in the community, types of communities at various Bible times, methods of armament, trade and money systems, the Jewish religion, other religions for various Bible times, captivities, social customs, eating customs, laws, geography of different Bible stories, and so forth. The particular information needed to explain, emphasize, or create greater lesson understanding can then be reported on by individual groups during the lesson presentation.

Churches often have reference books available. If not, most pastors have a few basic books they may be willing to lend. If your church doesn't have any reference books, and your pastor prefers not to lend his, try the community library—many have a good selection. *Reader's Digest* and *National Geographic* have very nice, picture-laden books that are helpful for children's reference projects.

For further research ideas, see the section on research.

Drama

Drama may be simple or complicated. Children may be involved in portions or in the total presentation. Adults may act out some of the characterizations. Costumes may be used. Drama may be informal, or it may be planned to include art and music. For some specific lesson ideas, see the section on drama.

Although not strictly drama, the lesson could be presented as if through the eyes of a newspaper, television, or radio reporter. Portions of the lesson are typed ahead of time and given to children for presession practice. These typed portions answer questions a reporter might ask. The reporter carries and uses a microphone head to add a semblance of reality.

Even a small scene presented in a basically lecture-type lesson makes the presentation *seem* different to the children.

Puppets

Puppets really belong in the category of drama. However, they can be inserted in a lesson portion for a brief time without being a major production. Puppets may be simple, made by children, and used to act out parts of the lesson. See the title page for the puppet section with more ideas. The last part of the section gives instructions on how to turn a Sunday-school lesson into a puppet script. The same principle may be used for changing a lesson into a drama.

Rearranging the Room

Altering the seating arrangements, table placement, or door openings does not restructure lesson type. It does give a feeling of change and adds interest in what is going to happen. That alone makes a difference when lessons follow the same basic pattern Sunday after Sunday.

Chairs may be shaped in seasonal patterns such as a heart or Christmas tree. They may be shaped according to some mode of travel mentioned or implied in the lesson. Chairs may be placed in the shape of an airplane. They may be shaped like a ship or an animal. Here are a few sample arrangements.

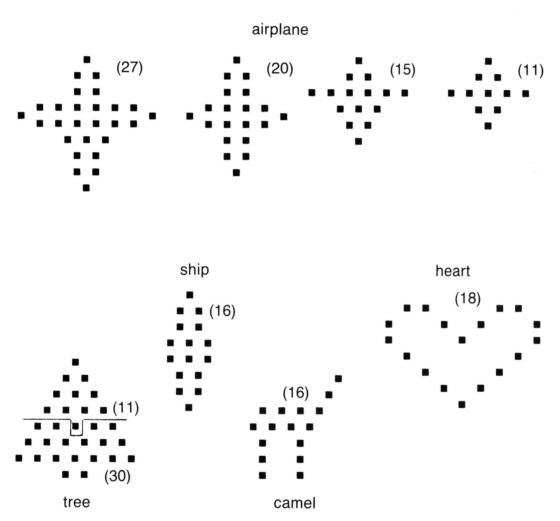

airplane

(27) (20) (15) (11)

ship (16)

heart (18)

tree (11) (30)

camel (16)

These shapes *(as with airplane example)* may be adapted to fit the number of students in your group.

If the lesson mentions or could have occurred in a tent, make the doorway look like a tent opening. Old sheets can be draped on either side of the doorway or opening. Spring-loaded curtain rods can be used at the top of the doorway for the sheets. In a lesson about Aquila and Priscilla, a sign may be placed by the door saying, "Tents by Aquila and Priscilla." Place a chair or canvas stool by the door opening. The result makes the children feel as if they are entering a place of business instead of their usual, ordinary room.

Adding sound effects to a change in seating creates interest and student involvement. If the story is about Jonah, place chairs in a shipshape. Have children make storm sounds and rock back and forth as if the ship is shaken by waves. Some child may be chosen to be the unfortunate Jonah. That child could be tossed overboard *(in a gentle pretense)*. Children as old as third and fourth graders enjoy making noise as part of sound effects. Airplane shapes make flying noises. Camels and other beasts of burden make noises, too.

With altered seating or room arrangements and with children making noises, pupils are physically involved in a lesson portion. Each bit of involvement gives the lesson and Bible truth more impact in the child's mind.

Creative Writing

Older children may enjoy making a newspaper page of events in or leading up to the lesson story. Children can work in small groups on one particular aspect of the story. They may need adult supervision. All the articles are typed during the week on a page in newspaper format. The following Sunday all will enjoy reading each other's articles, and, in effect, teach each other the lesson.

Other ideas for creative writing for a variety of ages may be found in the section on creative writing.

Games

When children are told lesson information will be used in a game following instruction time, they will often pay closer attention to the theme and details. This method doesn't really change lesson type or presentation, but it does alter the usual structure in the child's mind enough to add variety.

The questions may be based on events, people, places, things, motives, results, etc. in the story. The game may be one of the many given in the game section, such as Human Tick-Tack-Toe, Bible Spelldown, Bible Bowling, and so forth.

Charades may be used by adults or children to portray a portion of the lesson. Even a minor change, such as a short charade, breaks the monotony of the basic lecture-type presentation.

Art

If you know someone talented enough to draw pictures as they teach, ask them to present an occasional lesson. The children will enjoy both the art and the lesson.

Information from the lesson may be used for art projects when the lesson is finished. A collage about the basic theme, a peep show portraying a story scene, a model of the temple, or a simple crayon drawing reinforces and involves the student in knowledge and ideas presented during instruction time.

Those Beginning Steps

For some, the beginning steps toward being creative in academic and supportive activities may simply mean gathering the confidence to try some of the ideas suggested in the teacher's manual.

For others, it may mean adapting ideas suggested by the manual or other teachers.

Still others may begin to try new approaches offered by this book or other educational literature.

A tiny tot takes his first steps a few at a time. He often holds onto the sofa or coffee table as he tries to balance. Some of his efforts end in bumps on the floor. With each attempt, though, he gains in strength and confidence.

So it is with us as we develop creative ability and talent. It is not necessary to attempt something new in each aspect of the Sunday-school hour every Sunday. As you gain experience and confidence, you will find yourself increasing the challenge and difficulty in what you plan.

Don't expect everything of yourself at once. An old saying is appropriate here. "The longest journey begins with a single step." Journeys take time. So does the development of skills and talents.

Competent pianists have behind them years of practice, dedication, and effort. They needed the help of teachers, parents, and friends to reach the goals they set for themselves.

Being a successful and creative teacher is very similar to being an accomplished musician. We need the help of teachers and friends. We need to be dedicated in service to the Lord. We must remind ourselves occasionally that practice and effort polish and perfect skills. We could no more expect ourselves to play Beethoven's Third Symphony during our first piano lesson than we should expect ourselves to be a fascinating and creative teacher in our first attempts.

Most of us have goals. These goals may vary for the different areas of our lives. Many of these goals are lifelong in scope. All of life is a growing, reaching forward process. We may never totally experience some of our objectives. We will, however, move forward in growth and ability by striving to reach them.

Remember to be as loving, understanding, supportive, and forgiving of yourself as God commands us to be of others. It takes time and practice. You may have ability that will remain undiscovered if you allow yourself to become discouraged too easily.

This book is full of ideas and suggestions. Use those you like to stimulate and enrich your new beginnings. May God bless and inspire you as you work in the field of Christian education.

PUZZLES

On the following pages, you will find many ways to make puzzles.

Puzzles may be used as a presession activity, as an aid for memory work, as an activity to finish the Sunday-school hour, and as extra practice for children who have finished the regular daily work. They may also be used in special activity notebooks or booklets.

Puzzles may be decorated in a variety of ways. They can have a border drawn around them as this page does. *(The next section of this book gives many sample borders you may trace.)* Puzzles can have a flannelgraph picture from the lesson placed beside them—and be xeroxed. They may be decorated with pictures drawn like those in children's books. They can be made inside a shape traced from a coloring book. They can be shaped for different seasons—such as heart shape, star, Christmas tree, and so on. They can have a picture traced on them from the day's Sunday-school paper.

Make one master copy of the puzzle—complete with directions, puzzle, answers *(if you wish them to be on the master copy),* and decorations. This master copy is then reproduced. If the local church does not have machines for reproduction, find a business and office supply store. They often make copies for a cheaper price than copiers located in a store or library.

If the puzzle type is new to you, and you experience difficulty understanding how to make it, work the puzzle sample in the book. Once you solve a puzzle, it is easier to make.

There are many other kinds of puzzles besides the ones given here. These will give you an idea of how to make puzzles—and spark ideas of your own.

Letter Cross-out Puzzle

1. Space out the letters of the Bible verse or message so one, two, or three letters can be added between.
2. Use only one or two other letters between the original letters so it won't be too complicated to remember which letters to cross out.
3. Be certain to use only letters that are not in the puzzle message for crossing out, or you will cross out part of the message.
4. Directions may be as follows:

   "Cross out all the letter *Z* 's *(or the letters B and C—whatever works out for the puzzle)*. Now write the remaining letters in order on the lines below to make today's Bible verse."

   Message—Jesus loves you and me.

   Coded version 1—ZJZZEZSZZUZZSZLZZOZVZZESZYZOZUZZAZ ZNZDZZZMZZEZZ.

   Coded version 2—JCBESCUBSCBLCOBVCEBSCBYBOBUCABNBDC CMCBEBBC.

   "_____ _____ _____ _____ ___."

5. If the message or verse is long, it can be placed around the edge of the paper within lines like a frame. Lines for the puzzle can be placed inside this border with the directions, and possibly a picture if there is room. See example #5.

6. The message for this type of puzzle can also be placed in a circle with a picture in the center. Directions and lines for the message can be placed below the circle. See example #6.

7. In the same way, the puzzle can also be placed in a triangular shape. See example #7.

8. By varying the shape and arrangement of this type of puzzle, it can be used several times in a quarter.

Example #5

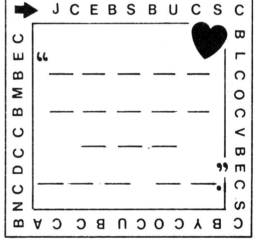

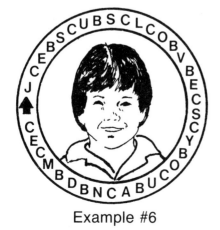

Example #6

Example #7

21

Alternating Letter Puzzles

For this type of puzzle, a random letter is inserted between each letter of the verse.

1. Space out the letters of the Bible verse or message so one letter can be placed between each verse letter.
2. Write out the puzzle on student master copy.
3. Put directions on copy. Directions may read like this:
   "Beginning with the second letter, cross out every other letter. Then write the letters that are left in order on the lines below the puzzle."

Message—J E S U S L O V E S Y O U A N D M E.
Coded version—JAEZSOULSILPOCVWEDSPYAOXUFARNZDHMRE.
"__ __ __ __ __   __ __ __ __ __   __ __ __   __ __ __   __ __ ."

Scrambled Words Puzzle

1. Take the words of the Bible verse or message and scramble the letters in each word.
2. Keep the words spaced apart and in the original order of the verse.
3. Directions might read something like this:
   "Unscramble each word in the puzzle. When you have each word unscrambled, put it on the line for that word below the puzzle."

Message—Jesus loves you and me.
Scrambled version—esJsu sevol oyu dan em.
"_____   _____   _____   _____
_____ ."

Missing Letters Puzzle

1. Write out the words of the puzzle on practice copy.
2. Then leave out certain letters. It usually works best to leave out the vowels.
3. Set up on master copy with the letters missing and give the directions.
4. Directions may read like this:
   "Fill in the missing letters to make the Bible verse for today."
   Message—Jesus loves you and me.
   Puzzle version—J__S__S L__V__S Y__ __ __ND M__ .

Secret Codes

There are several types of codes to use for Bible verses or messages from lessons. One can use a number code, a symbol code, a letter code, Morse code, or a picture code.

1. Write out the verse or secret message.
2. Assign symbols, letters, numbers, or pictures to replace the original words or letters of the verse or message.
3. Write directions and give code explanation.
4. Make lines for the words of the verse or message.
5. Put the symbol, letter, number, or picture under each line to replace the original letter or word.
6. If you wish, leave room for a decorative border or picture on the finished copy.

Older children enjoy trying to work out the code. Simply make the puzzle as directed above but omit the explanation of the code.

Number Codes

1. Follow the general directions given for secret codes.
2. Write out the verse and the alphabet.
3. Check the verse for the letters of the alphabet that appear in it. Look for the letters in alphabetical order so you won't leave out any. For example, see if the verse contains the letter *a.* If it does, assign the number 1 to the letter *a.* Then look for the letter *b* in the verse. If there is no letter *b*, skip that letter and look for the letter *c.* When you find the letter *c*, assign to it the number 2.
4. Cross out each letter in the alphabet and the verse as you work your way through them setting up the code.

Verse or message—Jesus loves you and me.
Alphabet—A B C D E F G H I J K L M N O P Q R S T U V W X Y Z
Code—A = 1 D = 2 E = 3 J = 4 L = 5 M = 6 N = 7 O = 8 S = 9 U = 10 V = 11
Y = 12

"___ ___ ___ ___ ___ ___ ___ ___ ___ ___ ___ ___ ___ ___ ___ ___ ___ ___."
  4   3   9 10   9   5   8 11   3   9   12   8 10   1   7   2   6   3

This type of code works well with any age from first grade on up. For children in the first through third grades, it is easier than some of the more difficult codes.

Symbol Code

1. Write out each letter that appears in the verse.
2. Assign each letter a symbol.

This type of code is better for children from third grade on up. Children of this age have more mature visual/perceptual skills, and they don't get as confused with small symbols of a similar type.

Verse or message—Jesus loves you and me.

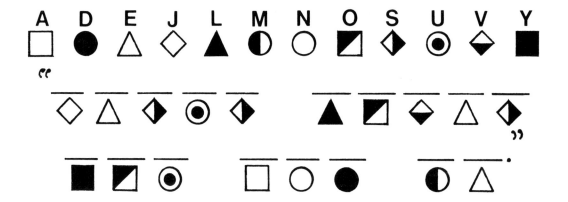

Morse Code

1. Follow the general guidelines given in the opening section of secret codes.
2. Use this type of code with older children who will not be visually confused by the many dots and dashes.

Verse or message—Jesus loves you and me.

A ·- B -··· C -·-· D -·· E · F ··-· G --· H ···· I ·· J ·--- K -·- L ·-·· M -- N -· O ---
P ·--· Q --·- R ·-· S ··· T - U ··- V ···- W ·-- X -··- Y -·-- Z --··
Numerals: 1 ·---- 2 ··--- 3 ···-- 4 ····- 5 ····· 6 -···· 7 --··· 8 ---·· 9 ----· 0 -----

" ___ ___ ___ ___ ___
 ·--- · ··· ··- ···

___ ___ ___ ___ ___ ___ ___ ___
·-·· --- ···- · ··· -·-- --- ··-

___ ___ ___ ___ ___ ."
·- -· -·· -- ·

Letter Codes

1. One way to do this type of code is to reverse the alphabet.
Verse or message—Jesus loves you and me.
Code—

    A B C D E F G H I J K
    L M Z Y X W V U T S R Q
    P O N N O P Q R S T U V
    W X Y Z M L K J I H G F
    E D C B A

" ___ ___ ___ ___ ___   ___ ___ ___ ___ ___   ___ ___ ___
  Q V H F H   O L E V H   B L F

___ ___ ___   ___ ___ ."
 Z M W   N V

2. Another way to do a letter code is to use two letters together for the secret symbol.

24

Verse or message—Jesus loves you and me.

Code—A = zy D = xw E = vu J = ts L = rq M = po N = nm O = lk S = ji U = hg
V = fe Y = de

" __ __ __ __ __ __ __ __ __
    ts vu ji hg ji rq lk fe vu ji

__ __ __ __ __ __ __ __."
dc lk hg zy nm xw po vu

Picture Code

1. Picture codes can be done with stickers or seals that replace the individual letters or words for a verse or message.
2. Put the verse in picture code on a large poster. Under the verse place lines for the words and a code explanation.
3. Each child can have an answer sheet with directions. He can work the code from the master chart.
4. This would work well with younger children.

E J L M O S U V

Using a Grid

A grid is a network of evenly spaced horizontal and perpendicular lines. It looks something like a piece of graph paper with larger than normal squares.

A grid made of heavy, dark lines is very useful in providing even spacing for placement of letters in certain types of puzzles.

When a plain, lightweight white paper is placed over the grid, the lines and spaces show through. You only need to use an area the size appropriate for your puzzle. Make certain you leave room on the page for directions and clues.

Crossword puzzles A grid provides both lines and spaces for any size crossword puzzle.

Word Search puzzles Lines are not necessary for this kind of puzzle. However, precise spacing is a must for the word search puzzle to work. The grid placed under the puzzle page being prepared assures accuracy.

Grid puzzles Certain kinds of puzzles are made in large grids. A word or phrase is placed inside each square. Letters and numbers help the student coordinate words into the Bible verse or message.

Computer Circuit or *Bionic Circuit puzzles* Grid squares the size of the ones on this page could be helpful in making the circuit squares for this type of puzzle.

Words Run Together puzzle A grid square this size works well for this type of puzzle.

Word Line Maze and *Word Chase puzzles* It is much easier to set these puzzles up accurately with a grid page placed underneath the page on which you are constructing the puzzle.

Grids for game use An overhead transparency of a plain grid works well for playing Bible Scrabble.

(Permission is granted to copy both in xerox and transparency form the grid provided at the end of the puzzle section.)

Word Search

Word search puzzles can be used for any lesson or theme. They can be used to review books of the Bible, names of disciples, words in a Bible verse or message, or names of places, things, or people.

This type of puzzle can be made into different shapes for various seasons such as tree shape—Christmas, heart shape—Valentine's Day, leaf shape—fall; or it can be fitted into a picture shape—boy, girl, animal, etc.

1. When making this puzzle, be certain to leave enough room for the directions and the list of words to be used in the puzzle.
2. Place a blank piece of paper on a grid. *(Example given.)* The previous section also explains use of the grid.
3. In crossword fashion, use the words from your list. Keep puzzle as compact as possible.
4. Fill in the blank spaces that are left *(in whatever shape you are trying to create)* with unused letters from words in the list. Take care not to make any other words as you fill in the puzzle. Extra words might confuse the children.
5. Try to adjust the challenge level of the puzzle to the ability level of your class. For first through third grade, run the words from left to right and top to bottom. Older students like the challenge of backward words run from right to left, and words that run from bottom to top. Several verses may be used in puzzles for older children.
6. Directions might read:
   "Read the list of words for which you are searching. Circle each word as you find it in the puzzle. Cross each word from the list as you find it. The first one has been done for you."

1. List
   Peter
   Mark
   Paul
   John
   Luke

2. Grid example

3. Partial puzzle

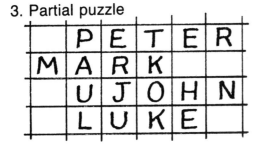

4. Finished puzzle

Cut and Paste Puzzle

1. Each child has a master sheet of paper that may have instructions, a picture to go with the lesson, and a section for the cut and paste words.
2. Each child is given an extra sheet of paper that contains the words to cut and paste.
3. The words to be cut out can be set up like a jigsaw puzzle, or they can be done in plain boxes of the same or varying sizes.
4. The master sheet has exactly the same shapes—only with the shapes in the correct order for the verse.
5. The place for the cut and paste words can form a shape to match the lesson. For instance: If the lesson is about feeding the five thousand, the place for the cut and paste words can be made into the shape of a basket. *(See example.)* If the lesson is about Josiah and the treasure chest for the temple, make the cut and paste section in the shape of the chest.
6. The directions may read like this:

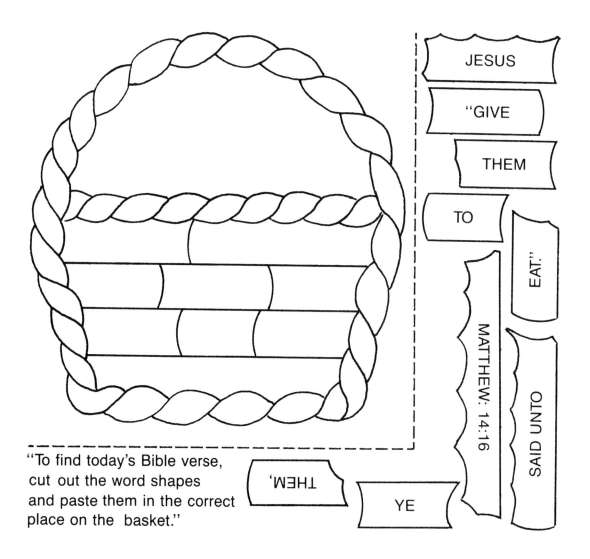

"To find today's Bible verse, cut out the word shapes and paste them in the correct place on the basket."

28

Crossword Puzzles

1. Write out the questions you wish to ask for the crossword puzzle. These may be for people, places, things, or word definitions. Usually the questions are set up for *Across* and *Down* answers.
2. Next place the answers crossword puzzle fashion on a page over a grid as was done for the word search puzzle. This gives you correct places to draw boxes for the children's answers.
3. Then number the questions and correlate the answers with the questions.
4. Put the questions down one side of the paper; put the crossword form without words on the other side.
5. Directions:
   "Write the answer to question 1 in the puzzle spaces with the same number. Do the other questions in the same way."

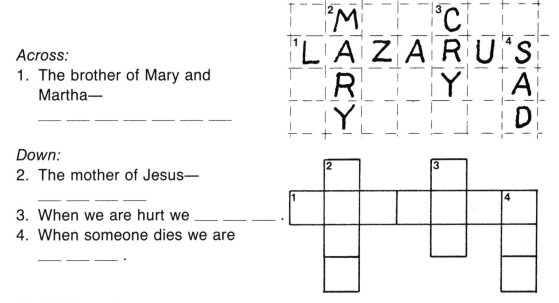

Across:
1. The brother of Mary and Martha—

   —— —— —— —— —— —— ——

Down:
2. The mother of Jesus—

   —— —— —— ——

3. When we are hurt we —— —— —— .
4. When someone dies we are

   —— —— —— .

Grid Puzzles

Coded Grid Puzzle

   This grid puzzle uses letters and numbers that intersect to give the location of the words of the Bible verse or message.

1. Draw a grid with enough squares for all the words in the verse or message. This type of puzzle needs a long verse to be effective.
2. Try to find a verse that will fit into a grid of three squares by five squares *(a fifteen word verse)*, a grid of four squares by four squares *(a sixteen word verse)*, a grid of four squares by five squares *(a twenty word verse)*, or a grid of five squares by five squares *(a twenty-five word verse)*. If the verse you are using does not fit into a grid of this sort—by word count—and you need more words, simply add the number of words you need by using random words. Then don't use the code numbers for the random words when working out the answer lines.

3. Make the squares in the grid large enough for the length of the longest word. If the longest word is a word like "everybody," make the squares tall enough so the word could be printed in this way: everybody.
4. Mix the words of the verse and place them in the squares.
5. Make lines below the puzzle for the words. Under the correct lines put the code for each word.
6. Directions may read:

   "Look at the first code symbol for the first line underneath this puzzle. On the puzzle grid, move your finger down to row C and then across to column 3. Put the word from that square in the grid on the first line. Do this with each of the codes and words until you have completed the verse. One has been done for you."

	1	2	3	4
A	AND	WILL	COURAGE	A
B	STRONG	FOR	NOT	FAIL
C	GOOD	LORD	BE	THEE
D	GOD	THE	OF	THEY

" BE _____ _____ _____ _____ _____ _____
 C-3   B-1   A-1   D-3   A-4   C-1

_____ . . . _____ _____ _____ _____
 A-3   B-2   D-2   C-2   D-4

_____ . . . _____ _____ _____ _____ ."
 D-1   A-2   B-3   B-4   C-4

Deuteronomy 31:6

Grid Puzzle—Odd-Even

In this grid puzzle, plan the size of the grid squares as you did for the puzzle on the preceding page. However, in this puzzle you will be using more than one word in the square. The number will also be in the square, so leave enough space for three lines or more of type on top of each other.

1. Make the grid size according to what you need for the verse. Double the number of spaces. Depending on which you decide to use—odd or even numbers to cross out—write the words from the verse one or two to a square. If you have chosen to cross out odd numbers, the words of the verse will be in the even numbered squares. In the odd numbered squares, use random words or another verse not related to the lesson.
2. When typing in the numbers, mix them up slightly so the students really have to look at each number. Otherwise, they will just color in every other square and the challenge is not as great.
3. It is better to use this type of puzzle with children of second grade or older. They must be able to understand the odd-even method of counting.
4. Directions could read:
   "To find the verse for today, use a crayon to color in all the even numbered boxes. *(Change the directions if you are coloring in odd numbered boxes.)* Write the verse on the lines under the puzzle."

1 If any	2 Jesus said	3 man be	5 in Christ,	4 I am
6 the truth	7 he is	8 the life	10 the way	9 a new
13 creature: old	12 no man	15 things are	17 passed away;	14 cometh unto
19 behold, all	16 the father	18 but by	20 me. Love,	21 things are
22 Jesus cares.	23 become new.	25 2 Corinthians 5:17		

" _____ _____ _____ _____ _____

_____ , _____ _____ _____ _____ _____

_____ : _____ _____ _____

_____ _____ ; _____ , _____

_____ _____ _____ _____ ."

___ ___ _____ _____ : _____

Jigsaw Puzzle
This puzzle type can be done several ways.
1. Each child can write the day's Bible verse on an 8½" x 11" *(or any convenient size)* piece of construction paper. Then each one cuts his paper into puzzle pieces. They exchange puzzles and try to put them together. Different color paper might be used for each puzzle.

2. The Bible verse is written on paper with jigsaw-like lines between the sections of the verse. A fairly long verse can be used for this. The whole page, uncut, is xeroxed. Then the student cuts the puzzle apart. Now the children try to see how quickly they can put the puzzle back together again.
3. The Bible verse is written on paper and cut into jigsaw-like pieces. These pieces are arranged randomly on the surface of a copy machine inside the 8½" x 11" area. Lower the cover of the machine and process copies of the puzzle. Each child gets a page. Children cut out the pieces and put them together to form the verse.

Computer Circuit

1. A small verse of thirty or thirty-five letters is best. Count the number of letters in the verse you plan to use.
2. Plan the circuit so it doesn't cross itself too many times, or it will confuse the children.
3. Draw the circuitry somewhat like the example given.
4. If the verse is too long for a circuit, put part of it on the answer portion of the page. See example.
5. For added effect, lines of the circuit may be traced in red, or the boxes may be filled in with red or yellow see-through ink. (Practical only for small groups.)

6. Directions may read: "Begin at start. Follow the line. Each time you come to a letter in a box, write it on the blank line in the answer space."

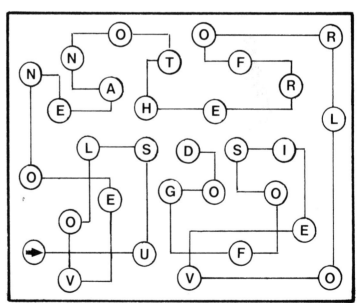

"Beloved, let __ __   __ __ __ __   __ __ __

__ __ __ __ __ __ __ : __ __ __ __ __ __ __

__ __   __ __   __ __ __ " (1 John 4:7).

Dot-to-Dot Puzzle

This type of puzzle can be used for many themes. If you can't find a picture like you want, you can make your own.

1. Take a ready-made dot-to-dot puzzle and type the words of a verse or message around its edges. *(See example.)*
2. If it is necessary to make your own puzzle, begin by putting dots around a picture from the lesson *(either person, thing, or animal).* Then draw or trace in the most important inner parts to make the puzzle plain. Now add the numbers and the words of the verse.
3. Directions may read like this:
   "With a pencil, connect the dots on the puzzle from one to forty. Then print the words in order on the lines beneath the puzzle."

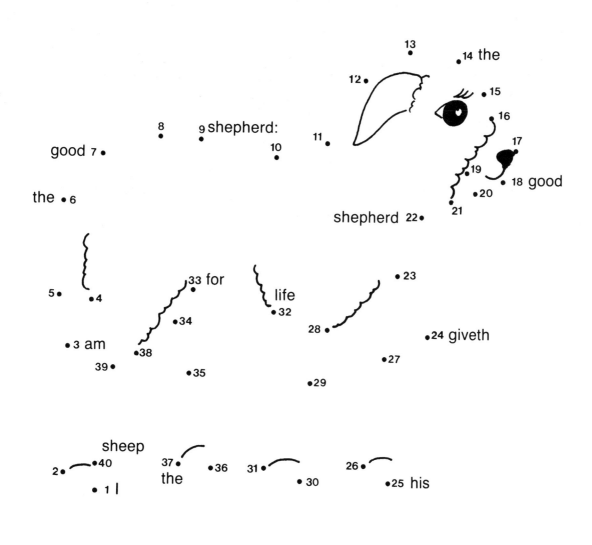

"_____ _____ _____ _____ _____ :

_____ _____ _____ _____ _____

_____ _____ _____ _____ " (John 10:11).

Stained Glass Window Puzzle

1. When planning puzzle size, be certain to leave enough room for instructions.
2. Draw outside edge or framework for puzzle according to the number of letters planned in the puzzle.
3. Write in block letters. You may put letters in less rigid form—flowing almost to blend into puzzle.
4. Place dots in each letter so children know what to color in.
5. Draw lines to connect the letters in the words. Make these lines resemble the letter lines so the puzzle is not too obvious.
6. Put a frame around the puzzle to resemble a picture frame. This will make your puzzle more decorative.
7. Directions may read:
   "Color in each dotted shape to find the verse" *(or word, message, etc.).*

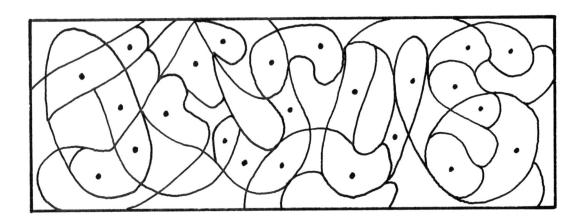

Words Run Together Puzzle

1. Make certain to leave room on the finished copy for directions. They may be worded this way:
   "Try to separate the line of letters into words to make today's Bible verse."
2. Age of child may vary this presentation a little. Younger children may need exact letter-spacing lines on which to write the letters to form words.

Puzzle example:
FORGODSOLOVEDTHEWORLDTHATHEGAVEHISONLYBEGOTTENSON

" ___ ___ ___ ___ ___ ___ ___ ___ ___ ___ ___ ___

___ ___ ___ ___ ___ , ___ ___ ___ ___ ___ ___ ___ ___ ___

___ ___ ___ ___ ___ ___ ___ ___ ___ ___

___ ___ ___ " (John 3:16).

3. Run together puzzles may also be done in squares with part of the message supplied in the answer portion.

4. Directions for this type of puzzle may read:
"Start with the first square. Follow the direction of the arrow. Then move across, up, down, or in whatever direction needed to make words. Fill in the blank lines. You will find the verse for today."

Puzzle example:
JESUS ___ ___ ___ ___

___ ___ ___ ___ ___ ___

___ ___ ___ ___ ___ ___ ___ ___ .

V	E	V	E	E
C	R	■	E	V
A	Y	O	N	A
M	E	T	O	S

Words Run Together and Symbol Combination

1. Choose two or three simple verses or messages.
2. Run the words together. Divide the letters into sets of one, two, or three letters—depending on how the puzzle comes out.
3. Give each message a symbol.
4. Prepare a grid. Fill in the grid with the segments of the puzzle messages and their symbols. Be certain to alternate from one message to another with the segments. Longer verses or messages may need to have their segments used more often.
5. Directions may read:
"Choose a symbol. Look for the squares with that symbol. Copy all the letters from these squares, in order. When you finish, divide the letters into words. You will find today's Bible verses."

%	+	*	%	+	*	%	+	*
JE	IW	JE	SU	IL	SU	SL	LT	SA
OV	RU	NS	ES	ST	WE	YO	IN	RS
UA	JE	PR	ND	SU	AY	ME	S	ER

% _____

+ _____

* _____

Words and Code Number Puzzle

This puzzle is similar to the Run Together and Symbol Combination on the preceding page except it uses whole words and a number for each verse. The words are mixed up and each is coded.

1. Choose three or four verses. If one or two are longer, simply use words from that verse more often on the grid, screen, or whatever style of presentation you choose.
2. This type of puzzle works well as a computer presentation.
3. Directions for this puzzle could be:

    "This computer has a secret Bible verse message for you. It is about working with God. *(Make the subject of that last sentence fit what your lesson is about.)* Choose one of the codes. Circle each word that has your code number. Then copy the words in order in the spaces given by the computer for your message. If you have time, you may do more than one secret message."

1	3	5	1		7		1
Be	Serve	We	strong		Whatsoever		and

3	7	5	7	3	1	7	3	5
the	ye	are	do	Lord	of	in	thy	laborers

7	3	1	7	3	5		1
word	God	a	or	with	together		good

7	1	3	1	3	7	1	3
deed	courage	all	for	thy	do	the	heart

7	7	1	3	5	1	7	3	1
all	in	Lord	and		with	thy	the	with	God

7	1	3	5	1	7	3	7	1
name	will	all	God	not	of	thy	the	fail

7	3		7
Lord	soul	thee	Jesus

COMPUTER MESSAGE:

_____
_____
_____
_____
_____
_____
_____
_____
_____
_____
_____

Code 1 - Deuteronomy 31:6
Code 3 - Deuteronomy 10:12
Code 5 - 1 Corinthians 3:9
Code 7 - Colossians 3:17

Maze

This type of puzzle can be used several ways. It can be a simple maze with directions such as this:

"Help the sheep find the sheepfold."

At the entrance of the puzzle, have a sheep, a boy, or whatever you need to follow your lesson theme. Another way to use this puzzle type is to have the words of a Bible verse strung out along the correct route. Other words chosen randomly are used along the false trails. You may have the student write the verse on lines at the bottom of the page. Mazes may be as complicated or as simple as you wish—depending on the age of the child working them. Mazes may be made of curved lines, straight lines, circles, or shapes for particular seasons—such as Christmas tree or star shape, heart shape, etc.

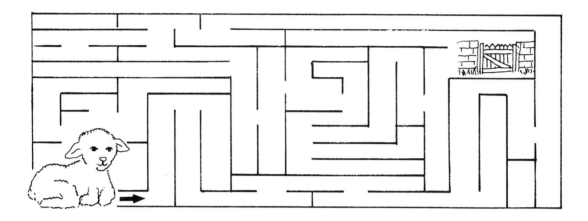

Word Line Maze

This puzzle looks like a word search puzzle at first glance. However, the words of the verse are in a sequence that can be followed by a line through the puzzle.

The words of the verse must be written on the page. Children need to know what the sequence of letters is so they can follow it with their pencils.

1. Put the letters of the words in a line sequence on paper laid over a grid.
2. Fill in the blank spaces with random letters.
3. Directions:

    "Beginning at the arrow, trace the words of this Bible verse through the maze."

Example for #1   Example for #2   Verse: "Be ye kind one to another" (Ephesians 4:32).

Answer

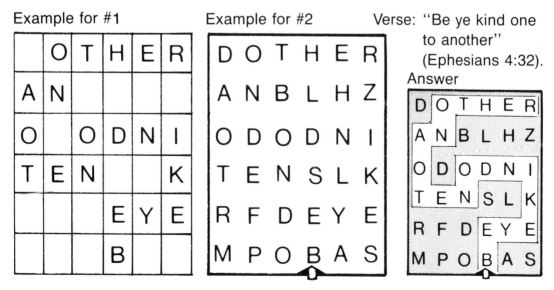

Word Chase

The word chase puzzle works on a similar principle as the *Word Line Maze*. The main difference in the two puzzles is that in *Word Chase* the new word begins with the last letter or two letters of the preceding word.

1. Use a grid underneath a plain piece of paper for accurate letter placement.

2. When you have chosen a general theme or topic for the puzzle, make a list of likely words for the theme. It often takes a little time and ingenuity to find ten or fifteen words on one theme that will fit together.

3. Place the words on the page using the grid. You may wish to place them in a rectangular shape—such as the puzzle example. Or, you may wish to put them in a particular shape.

4. A word chase puzzle does not give exact answers for which to look. It gives the first word. After that, only answer lines, first letter clues, or number of letters in the word given in parentheses ( ) at the end of the line are given. Look for the first word given. When you have found that word in the puzzle, work from there.

5. Directions may read as follows:
"The first word is given. Each new word starts with the last letter of the previous word. The lines below the puzzle show in parentheses ( ) the number of letters in the word for which you are looking. When you find the words, write them on the lines."

BIBLE PLACES

E	E	L	I	L	A	G	L	M	N	O	P
P	D	R	O	M	E	F	R	O	B	A	T
H	S	J	K	G	O	Z	E	Q	A	A	R
E	R	L	Y	A	S	T	D	E	R	U	V
S	H	P	S	K	E	W	S	A	X	H	M
U	T	A	R	S	U	S	R	Y	L	B	T
S	A	M	A	R	I	A	Z	S	H	Q	R

Clues:

_____ (4), E_____ (5), _____ (6),
[A three word place]

_____ (3), _____ (2), _____ (7),
_____ (7), _____ (7), _____ (6),
_____ (5), [A two word place]

_____ (3) _____ (3).

38

Quotation Unscramble

This unscramble puzzle gives all the letters in rows at the bottom that are needed for the verse. The top part of the puzzle looks like a crossword puzzle without the numbers. However, the words do not intersect to make other words as in a true crossword.

1. Place blank paper over a grid for accurate column and square placement.
2. Work out a verse—preferably short—that can be fitted into this semi-grid format. The puzzle may be as many squares wide as the paper if necessary. It may be three to ten rows high. More than three or four rows, however, make too difficult a puzzle for younger children.
3. Leave enough room on the paper for directions and verse reference.
4. When the verse is worked out in the fashion you see in the example, scramble the letters in the first column and place them in the open column under the squares. Do the second column in the same way, and so on until the puzzle is finished.
5. Leave upper squares empty for students to fill in.
6. Directions may read:

    "The letters in each column belong in the boxes just above them. They may not be in just the right order. Do not use the letters in the column more than once. When done, you can read a verse from the Bible."

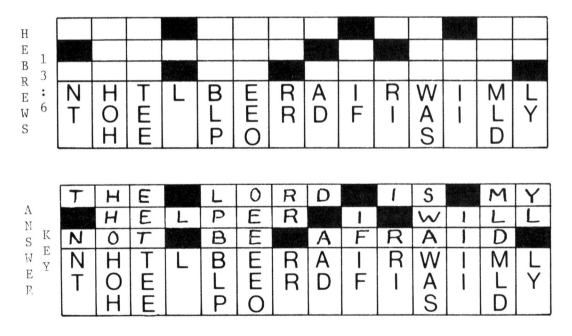

Acrostics

Word Acrostic

This puzzle hinges on a word spelled vertically. Other words—fill-ins for sentences given—are laid out horizontally.

1. Choose a word that is key to the basic theme of the other words to be given as fill-in answers.
2. Write the key word vertically. List as many words relating to the general

theme as possible. Plan a horizontal word for each letter of the verticle word. Choose words from the list to match key word letters.

3. Make up fill-in sentences for the words chosen.
4. Make a diagram for the verticle word and lines for the horizontal words.
5. Directions may read:

"Fill in the blanks in each numbered sentence with a word which makes sense. Put that word in the puzzle on the lines following the same number as the sentence. When you have finished, you will find six words that tell what Christ does for us."

Sentences:

1. A kind person
   ___ ___ ___ ___ ___ others.
2. God's Word ___ ___ ___ ___ ___ ___ ___
   us how to live.
3. Jesus ___ ___ ___ ___ ___ ___ ___ ___
   our sins.
4. A mother ___ ___ ___ ___ ___
   for her child.
5. Jesus sits on the right hand
   of the Father and
   ___ ___ ___ ___ ___ ___ ___ ___ ___ for us.
6. The Son of God
   ___ ___ ___ ___ ___ us from our sins.

Acrostic:

4 C ＿ ＿ ＿ ＿
1 H ＿ ＿ ＿ ＿
3 ＿ ＿ R ＿ ＿ ＿ ＿ ＿
5 I ＿ ＿ ＿ ＿ ＿ ＿ ＿ ＿
6 S ＿ ＿ ＿ ＿
2 T ＿ ＿ ＿ ＿ ＿

Fill-in answers: (1) helps, (2) teaches, (3) forgives, (4) cares, (5) intercedes, (6) saves

Verse Acrostic

Another type of acrostic looks like a crossword puzzle. Definitions are given as in a normal crossword, but answers are put in the blanks beside the definitions. Underneath each line is a number. That number coordinates with the letter in front of the word definition to help solve the puzzle.

Here's how:

In the crossword squares, letters and numbers are given. For example, A in a square refers to definition A. The number following A in the square represents one of the letters in the word defined.

Example: | A15 | A. Feline pet ___ ___ ___   (Answer—CAT)
                                                 67 37 15

In puzzle square A15, the letter needed to help make a word from the Bible verse would be letter T.

1. Choose a verse. Set it up to look like the upper part of Quotation Unscramble. Make squares ½″ x ½″ because both a letter and a number must go in the space with the answer.
2. Creating words and definitions:
   a. Write out all the letters in the Bible verse.
   b. Rearrange those letters into new words. Keep working until all the letters are used.
   c. Give a definition for each new word.
3. Assign each definition a letter. See sample puzzle.
4. Make lines for the number of letters in the answer for each definition.
5. Randomly assign numbers to each letter line.
6. Write in each puzzle square the letter and number for the alphabet letter needed to make a correct word answer. Refer to first example (A15).
7. Directions may read:
   "Write the correct word for each definition given below the puzzle. Match the number below each letter with the letter in front of the word definition. Now you have the code for filling in the squares. When the puzzle is filled in, a Bible verse can be read."

	B4	F31	I33	G35	F16	B20	I12		D1	F18	J17	
H40	E26	C38	E29		C6	H3	G30	D7		B36	B39	C23	I21
				F15	I42	D19		J11	B22	H32		E14	G8
C5	G2	A27	H9	A34	C13		A10	B25	D28		J41	A24	E37

(A) Wooden stockade ___ ___ ___ ___
                            10 24 27 34

(B) Discount certificate ___ ___ ___ ___ ___ ___
                                    4 25 36 39 22 20

(C) Place to sit ___ ___ ___ ___ ___
                   6 23 38 5 13

(D) Female horse ___ ___ ___ ___
                    19 1 28 7

(E) 60 minutes ___ ___ ___ ___
                 14 26 37 29

(F) Frozen rain __ __ __ __
15 31 16 18

(G) Rip or pull apart __ __ __ __
35 8 2 30

(H) 365 days __ __ __ __
40 9 3 32

(I) Choir activity __ __ __ __
33 42 21 12

(J) Common insect __ __ __
11 17 41

Picture Acrostic

In this puzzle, names of pictures are printed into squares or onto lines. The first letter of each picture word spells out another word. Children are asked to write them on the lines *(or in the boxes)* provided.

Pictures need not be elaborate.

Directions may read:

"Spell the word that names each picture. Write it in the boxes beside the picture. Then put the first letter of each word into the larger numbered boxes beside the puzzle. You will read a word that names someone who loves you."

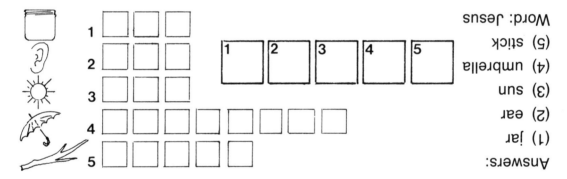

Letter Fill-in

All words to be filled in for this type of puzzle are on a central theme.

1. Make a list of all the words from the theme or verse.
2. Choose three—3 letter words, four—4 letter words, five—5 letter words, etc., to make the puzzle square.
3. Inside the square is a row of boxes for each word. Some of the letters have been filled in. The missing letters are posted in order beside one of the puzzle rows.
4. Directions may read:
   "Each set of letters in the left column will complete one word from a parable Jesus taught. *(See Scripture references.)* Write the letters in the empty boxes. Do not change the order of the letters. One has been done for you."

Bible References: Matthew 13:24-30 Matthew 13:1-9, 18-23 Matthew 13:45 Luke 15:1-7 Luke 18:1-8

1. P A		O	W	E	
2. E P	T		R	E	
3. S R		E		R	L
4. J G	S	H		E	
5. A S		U	D		E

Mystery Squares

All words in this puzzle relate to a verse or set of verses.

The challenge for the maker of this puzzle is to choose a key word *(whose letters will appear in the mystery squares)* and enough other theme-related words the same length that will contain one each of the needed letters for the key word.

1. Choose a key word—either the one word central theme or an important missing word from a Bible verse. When beginning to make this type puzzle, it is easier to choose a four or five letter word from a Bible verse.
2. Choose four—4-letter words *(or however many you plan to use)*.
3. Make two grid-type diagrams—one for the scrambled words and one for the students' answers.
4. In the answer grid, circle the square in each row that will contain the letter needed to make the mystery word.
5. Scramble the words. Place them in the diagram rows in the order needed to assure correct spelling of the mystery word.
6. Leave room on the page for instructions and a place for the mystery word—simple lines or blank lines in the Bible verse. See puzzle example.
7. Directions may read:

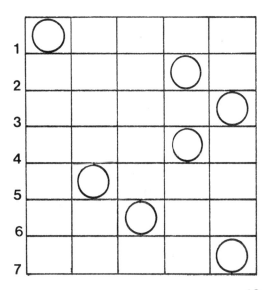

"Read Galatians 5:19-21 in the King James and Living Bibles. You will learn about the works of the flesh. Then unscramble each word in the puzzle square. Place each unscrambled word in the blank row with the same number. A mystery word will appear in the circles. Write that word on the blank lines in the Bible verse."

"Anyone living that sort of life will not

___ ___ ___ ___ ___ ___ ___ the kingdom of God" (Galatians 5:21, *Living Bible*)

Answers: 1-idols, 2-drunk, 3-flesh, 4-anger, 5-argue, 6-evils, 7-fight

Upside-Down Word

Words of this puzzle are printed upside down in a column. Underneath each column is a number. Below the sets of columns are blank lines with numbers for the student to write the word correctly. The number under each set of blank lines corresponds to the upside-down word in the column with the same number.

Directions might read:

"Each word in this puzzle has been written from bottom to top. As you read it, write the letters in the correct spaces on the numbered lines below the puzzle."

1	2	3	4	5	6	7	8	9	10	11	12	13	14	15
														E
										L				L
Y	C				L	R				L				P
E	I	D			L	U	D	D		A				O
B	Y	O	N		I	E	O	O	N	H	E	Y		E
O	M	V	A	I	W	B	Y	G	A	Y	S	B	M	P

" ___ ___ ___ ___ ___ ___ ___ ___ ___ ___ ___ ___ ___ , ___ ___ ___ ___ ___
      1   2   3   4   5

___ ___ ___ ___ ___ ___ ___ ___ ___ ___ ___ ___
    6   7   8   9   10

___ ___ ___ ___ ___ ___ ___ ___ ___ ___ ___ ___ ___ ___ . "
 11   12   13   14   15

Jeremiah 7:23

44

BORDERS

Borders may be used to emphasize directions, make a place for a student to drawn a picture, or to decorate a puzzle. They may be seasonal.

Permission is granted to trace any of the borders on these pages.

To trace a pattern, use lightweight white paper over the pattern page. If it is difficult to see the pattern under paper, hold up to a window and trace.

Picture Frame Borders
1. Trace the border, including corners.
2. Turn pattern page upside down. Trace second side and corners on other half of page. *(For patterns A, F, G, H, I, J, K, L, and M.)*
3. Place pattern on side to trace top and bottom, being careful to match with previously traced corners.

Example for #1	Example for #2	Example for #3

4. For patterns C, N, O, and P, use side A for the right side border. Use side B for the left side border. For pattern C, simply extend the bottom and top border given. For patterns N, O, and P follow step three above. With pattern O *(sunshine faces),* change direction of face after circles and sun rays are drawn.

Top-Bottom Borders
This type of pattern may be used to enclose a title. It may be used one-half on top of full page and one-half on bottom. It may be used just for top.

Corner Borders
Pattern is used just at corners. See pattern E. Any of these borders could be used just for corners.

Pattern C

Pattern D

Side B

Side A

Pattern E

Many of the short examples for border patterns in this chapter are used in longer form throughout the book.

You may wish to copy them.

When copying these short borders, first draw a faint line for border placement. Trace in the corners. Fill in sides by moving pattern along placement line as each segment is traced.

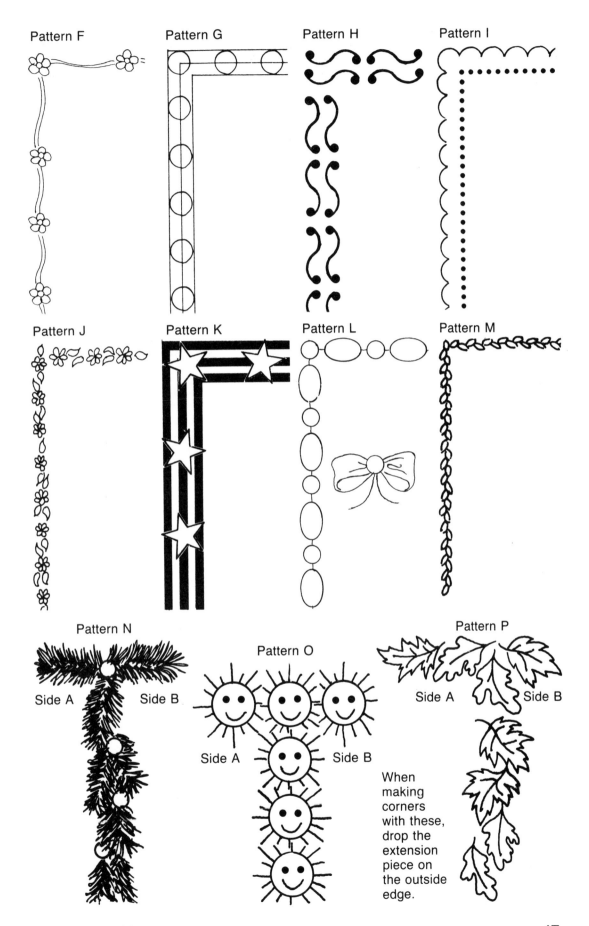

Pattern F

Pattern G

Pattern H

Pattern I

Pattern J

Pattern K

Pattern L

Pattern M

Pattern N

Side A   Side B

Pattern O

Side A   Side B

Pattern P

Side A   Side B

When making corners with these, drop the extension piece on the outside edge.

BULLETIN BOARDS

Bulletin boards are an attractive way to teach, decorate, record work, display art, and make children feel unique and important.

Boards may be three-dimensional, religious, secular, seasonal, or personal in children's activities. They may be as complicated or simple as you desire.

Most publishing companies repeat curriculum every year or two. Seasons roll around regularly. Each year you have new children who have not seen your materials. Most bulletin board supplies can be stored and reused. Multi-use of these materials makes the additional effort to prepare an attractive, effective board well worthwhile. Many hours of preparation time may be saved this way.

Ideas for boards may come from any part of life. Some boards may be adaptations of others you have seen in public schools, churches, magazines, and teacher's manuals.

Storage may be as simple as folding butcher paper to make envelopes, stapling sides, inserting materials to be stored, labeling envelopes, and standing upright in a deep drawer or cardboard box on a shelf.

Bulletin boards are truly friends. Occasionally, let children supply part of what is put up either in artwork or help. Make the boards relevant to the quarter's theme, yet changeable enough to retain freshness. If you do, you have saved time and created an effective teaching tool.

The atmosphere of the Sunday-school room is often set by what the children first see as they enter. The attractive use of color, ideas, and student work will reach out and welcome.

Teaching With Bulletin Boards

Bulletin boards do not have to be big, empty, intimidating spaces. They can be an integral part of teaching. If wisely used, bulletin boards are fresh, review learning, have continual interest to the student, cause him to act on information taught in the lesson, and provide some presession activities to relate to the lesson.

Involving children in the preparation of bulletin boards can have an even greater impact than reinforcing learning. Some boards can build a child's self-esteem and self-confidence, his faith and understanding, and his confidence of his value in the group. Children *(and adults)* like to see their names listed in positive situations, see their work displayed, and receive praise and recognition. In assembling bulletin boards with children, the teacher has one more opportunity to interact and touch the lives of those children. Each student/teacher contact further opens communication lines to reiterate the child's special place in the group and his personal importance. The warmth of the teacher, the physical touches given in pats of encouragement and hugs of appreciation, the words of thanks or friendship will strengthen the child's desire to be in a church learning situation, and it will encourage him to serve the Lord.

Specific Bulletin Board Uses

Record Keeping Boards
Attendance, memory work, or Sunday-school offering contests and activities provide ideal bulletin board material. These can be done as simple displays added to each week or as games. The charts and stickers used for some may be purchased at educational supply stores. See the chapter on Memory Work for two examples.

Art Display
Boards may display children's art projects relating to their work. This reinforces the learning and repetition provided by that activity in the first place. Children may be given art projects specifically designed to fit a theme such as Easter, Christmas, or Valentine's Day.

Teaching Tool
This kind of board may emphasize some lesson unit or quarter's theme. Picture sets such as those by Richard Hook pertaining to the Easter season work well. With the rotation of pictures on the board, a subject is usable for many Sundays.

Birthday Party Board

A decorative board to announce those having birthdays during the quarter is good for a month. It can be put up three weeks before the actual day for special recognition, cupcakes, juice, or games. If the Sunday-school class is small, use the board every six months instead of quarterly.

Gift wrap may be used as the background. Put names on white or colored 3″ x 5″ cards. Gift wrap curl tie in several colors, draped here and there over the board, adds visual interest.

Another way to prepare a birthday board is to use scratch and sniff certificates. Use a plain background of a color to accent a color in the certificates. Children take the certificates home as their card from the Sunday school when the party is over. These may be purchased at educational supply stores.

Activity Display Board

Color photographs used to highlight special group activities *(picnics, award ceremonies, field trips, swimming parties, summer or snow camps, and so on)* get much attention when posted on a board. Children love to look at themselves.

Seasonal Display

Items relating to seasons may be used in many ways. Art or educational stores carry pictures, shapes, and patterns usable for Sunday school or church bulletin boards. Natural items *(leaves, shells, etc.)* may be used. Children are taught to value and appreciate God's world.

Coloring books sometimes have pictures children can color, cut out, and use. Christian book stores carry Christian theme coloring books and wall murals. These could be colored and used for bulletin boards.

Creative Writing Display

Stimulate enthusiasm for creative writing by displaying work on attractive boards. See Creative Writing chapter in this book for suggestions.

Bulletin Board Supplies

Backgrounds

Backgrounds may be made of colored burlap, colored or plain bulletin board paper, colored flannel, gift wrap paper—plain or printed, old sheets—white or colored, butcher paper, purchased corrugated bulletin board liner, construction paper, or old newspapers.

Borders

Borders may be:

1. Paper cut into shapes along one side such as: scallops, fringe, icicles, triangles, etc.
2. Artwork done by students: construction paper leaves, hearts, snowflakes, shamrocks, handprints, and so on
3. Purchased borders—can be found in educational supply stores
4. Twisted crepe paper streamers (*1/2" width is easier to pin or staple and doesn't crush as easily*)
5. Braid or rope
6. Artificial flowers and leaves

Letters

The quality of lettering affects the entire appearance of the board. Letters may be made from patterns. They can be purchased to match borders that are made by several companies. If there is extra border in the package, letters can be cut from it to save purchasing them. Letters may also be written on rectangular pieces of paper with felt-tip pens. If neatly done, these title or informational signs can save a lot of cutting and pinning.

Yarn, braid, or thin rope glued to paper or pinned to the board serve as letters.

How to Copy Letter Patterns

Lay a page with letter patterns over a piece of tagboard the same size. Insert a sheet of carbon paper, carbon side down, between. Trace with heavy strokes over the letters. Cut out tagboard patterns. Trace around patterns on colored construction paper. Cut out construction paper letters. Save the tagboard patterns and reuse. Tagboard is the type of paper from which manila folders are made.

Three-Dimensional Effect

This effect is achieved by using leaves, branches, artificial flowers, folded or scored paper, or other natural items. Letters, leaves, and shapes of all sorts can be pinned to a board. When pulled out slightly toward the pin heads, a three-dimensional effect is created.

Almost any item can be attached to a bulletin board by slant pinning around the article. Branches can be attached by pinning through the bark.

How to Enlarge Patterns

Few churches have opaque projectors—machines in which pages may be placed and projected on a screen or wall in larger size. Many public schools have them. Some schools will allow them to be used on their premises.

Small, inexpensive plastic enlargers may be purchased through retail stores' catalog departments. These work well for small pictures and most items an average church worker would use.

An overhead projector can be used, however, on the same principle as the opaque projector for enlarging. Make an overhead transparency of the page of patterns or an entire bulletin board sketch. *(If a transparency making machine is not available, simply lay a clear transparency over the pattern page. Trace patterns with a washable overhead pen.)* Place the transparency on the projector. Focus the pattern outlines in the size you wish. Patterns may be made smaller or larger by moving the projector—close-up for smaller pictures, back for larger pictures. Project patterns onto a bulletin board or wall. Trace pattern on paper with a pencil or felt-tip pen. *(When using felt-tip pens, put two layers of paper under the tracing area. Ink from these pens may seep through the paper and mark the wall.)*

It is helpful to enlarge pictures on the bulletin board to be used. In this way, exact sizing and object placement is easier.

ART

Art is not just an end product. Experimenting, creating, and discovering reinforce and extend learning. Art often provides the "doing" which brings about "understanding."

Art projects may just be a creative activity to round out the Sunday-school program. However, such projects mean a great deal more if related to the Sunday-school lesson or quarter's theme.

Children's art may be incorporated into bulletin boards. It can be used as lesson, unit, or quarterly reviews. Art projects can be an expression of love when given away as part of a "helping others" unit, or for Mother's Day, Father's Day, or Grandparents' Day. Art may be included as part of music or creative writing.

Increased understanding of how people lived, worked, and worshiped in Bible times may come from such things as paper sculpture villages, cloth model of the temple, bulletin boards about jobs in Bible times—such as a shepherd. Children may make sheep for the board. These activities and others like them involve research and Bible study as well as art.

Puppets may be used in many ways after they have been an art project. See the section about puppets in this book.

A great deal of art and personal involvement develop around dramatizing Bible stories. See the chapter about drama.

As a child lives with a banner made in Sunday school, Bible truth is reinforced over and over and learning is greatly extended.

A teacher may *teach*, but until a child can incorporate and experience that teaching in positive life changes, he hasn't *learned*. Art provides a child with the first step of acting on what he has learned and making it part of himself.

The following pages give information about a variety of art processes. They suggest possible lesson uses for some of them. Use them as a key to open the door for new ideas of your own.

Crayons

Crayons are the most useful and versatile art tool available. Crayons may be used to color pictures already prepared by a publisher. They may be used on a piece of plain paper, or inside a teacher drawn border.

The fine muscular motor coordination in a child's hand is not fully developed in the preschool, kindergarten, and first grade years. Educators recommend using the fat crayons in the eight primary colors for children of this age.

Crayon Rubbings

Lay medium to lightweight paper over the back of a heavily veined leaf. Use old crayons or crayons with the paper covering removed. Lay crayon on its side. Rub crayon across the paper over the leaf until shape and texture of veins show clearly. Use different types of leaves placed in different places under the paper. Use a new color for each leaf.

Crayon Resist

Color a design or picture on a piece of paper. Make a light mixture of black tempera paint, or use regular strength dark watercolors. Paint over entire page, including picture. Crayon picture will resist the paint wash.

This type of picture works well for illustrating a Bible story that takes place at night, in a storm, or in water *(light blue color wash)*.

Crayon Etchings

Using light colored crayons, entirely cover surface of paper with a variety of colors. Using black crayon, color over the entire surface of previously colored paper. Scratch a picture lightly with a nail. If the pressure on the nail is correct, the light colors will show through.

Crayon Stained Glass Window

Grate old color crayons on a vegetable grater. On several thick layers of old newspaper, lay a sheet of wax paper. Sprinkle crayon bits over the wax paper, either randomly or in a pattern. Lay another sheet of wax paper the same size as the first over crayon bits. Place a layer of old newspapers over the wax paper. Iron with a hot iron until the crayon bits melt. Stop before the wax paper melts! The iron should be used by an adult for younger children or supervised carefully with older children. Leave pictures in the layers of paper as they cool so they will not curl.

When pictures are completed, place in a construction paper frame and tape to a window so the light shines through the colors.

Prints

Paint to be used for printing can be any color tempera or poster paint. Mix and place in small shallow dishes for dipping.

Paper should be a durable type such as butcher paper or medium to heavyweight construction paper.

Vegetable Printing

The potato is the best vegetable to use for printing because it is large enough to make a nice sized print, soft enough to carve without damage to little fingers, and porous enough to hold paint for a print or two.

Cut the potato in half crosswise. Carve the design desired. Dip in paint. Press onto the paper.

Children can cut a different design in the second half of the potato, or they can trade potato designs. They may use different colors.

Sponge Printing

Different size and texture sponge pieces may be used for this type of printing.

Dip sponge piece into paint, taking care not to saturate it. Children make several prints with the sponge and redip.

Thumb and Finger Printing

Use an office ink pad. Place thumb on pad and then on paper. These thumb or fingerprints may be used as a body base for little animals or bugs. The prints will make cute bees, spiders, mice, etc. See examples.

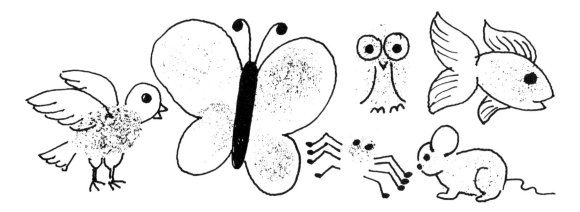

Hand Printing

Handprints may be made using tempera paint. When these have dried, they may be cut out.

Some uses for handprints:

1. A border for a bulletin board about helping others
2. Leaves on a tree *(if done in green)*
3. Petals around a sunflower
   Use a brown circle of construction paper the size of a saucer. Use yellow paint for the handprints. Glue the handprints by the palm around the brown circle.
4. A handprint on a Mother's Day card

Mobiles

Mobiles—pieces of metal or clay sculpture, natural objects, or paper pictures hung from wires or threads which are suspended from a hanger, stick, or wire frame. A mobile is usually hung in a place where the parts can be set in motion by air currents.

Mobiles are occasionally suggested as a craft activity for children's lessons. Some publishers even provide pictures in student books.

Collage

A collage is a composition—pieces of printed matter and pictures glued on another paper to make a picture with a unifying theme.

Old magazines and newspapers provide pictures and printed words for titles.

Many lesson themes could be reinforced with this art form. Examples:

- The fruit of the Spirit
  (pictures of fruit)
- Helping others
  (pictures of people in need)
- Our body, the temple of the Lord
  (pictures of good things to eat, exercise, etc.)
- Responsibility to those dependent on us
  (pictures of pets to be taken care of)
- Stewardship of God's world
  (pictures of things in nature)

- Stewardship—material things *(pictures of things we own, emphasis on tithing)*
- Witnessing *(pictures of people we could witness to)*
- Missions *(pictures of people from a race or continent being studied)*

Clay and Dough

Both clay and dough can be purchased for children to use.

Younger children like to work with clay anytime. Older children enjoy using clay if it is part of a specific project such as a diorama.

Following are several recipes for dough or clay if you prefer to make your own. Food coloring may be added to any of these recipes.

Sugar Dough

(for younger children who might take a nibble)

1 cup water

2 cups sugar

3 cups flour

Mix and knead. If dough is too stiff, add more water. Make into figures. If you wish to preserve them, bake in a low heat oven *(275-300°)* until hard. When cold, these may be painted or decorated. If sprayed with shellac or fixative, they will keep better. Dough will keep for a week or so in a tightly closed plastic container or ziplock bag. This dough is not as durable as the salt and flour kind, but it is safer for little ones.

Flour/Salt Clay

2 ½ cups flour

½ cup salt

3 tablespoons corn oil

1 tablespoon alum

2 cups boiling water

Mix ingredients well. Make hole in center. Add boiling water. Mix well. Store in closed containers.

Salt/Cornstarch Clay

2 cups salt

1 cup cornstarch

1 cup water

Mix. Cook over low heat until dough is stiff. Add a drop or two of cooking oil to slow drying of dough. When cool, shape into figures. Let dry a couple of days or heat in oven as in Sugar Dough recipe.

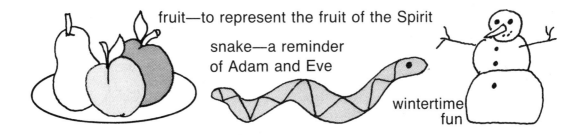

fruit—to represent the fruit of the Spirit

snake—a reminder of Adam and Eve

wintertime fun

Diorama

A diorama is a scenic representation where paper or sculptured figures and other lifelike details are displayed. These scenes are usually in miniature. Dioramas may be made using flannelgraph or figures cut from lesson papers. Scenery may be drawn for the background. *(Children could make the sculpt figures for the scene.)*

Peep Show

A peep show is a diorama in a shoe box.

Take the lid off the shoe box. Decorate the sides and back of the box to fit the scene or story you have in mind. Make an eye-sized hole in one end of the box. Tape light blue tissue paper over the box in place of the lid. One layer of tissue will allow light through but will give the effect of a peep show.

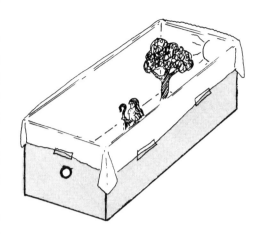

Children may replace the lid to protect the tissue paper when the box is not in use.

Displays

Whether on tables, placed on the wall, or pinned to a bulletin board, displays capture attention.

Displays may be made of things children bring or things the teacher has prepared.

Displays contain such things as:
- Photographs of children's activities *(field trips, picnics, class work, special church functions)*
- Awards earned by the children
- Pictures cut from magazines relating to a central theme
- Natural objects from God's world *(rocks, shells, leaves)*
- Easter or Christmas stand-up scenes
- Prizes for memorization or attendance contests
- Artwork done by children in relation to a particular lesson *(clay, sculpture, pictures)*
- Library of Christian children's books or comics

Finger Painting

Finger paint colors may be purchased. Good papers to use are plain white butcher or waxed butcher paper.

Young children have a lot of fun using *instant* pudding mixes. Mix the pudding as directed *(or a little bit thinner)*. For colors, use vanilla pudding mix and food coloring. For brown paint, use chocolate pudding mix. Children can lick their fingers when they get too sticky!

Have children bring an old shirt or blouse to wear for messy art projects like finger painting. If parents care to donate the shirts, they can be stored for future use.

When painting on paper, be certain children do not have too much paint or pudding mix. The paint will be too thick, will crack as it dries, and the picture will not be suitable for some of the following suggested projects.

Recipes for Finger Paint

1 cup cornstarch
¼ cup soap flakes
4 cups boiling water

Mix well. Add food coloring.

½ cup flour
2 cups warm water

Mix on high with electric beater or on whip in blender. Add food color or tempera paint powder and remix.

Uses for finger painted pictures:

1. Frame with white butcher paper or construction paper and hang.
2. Cut out shapes when the pictures are dry. These shapes could be seasonal:

    Christmas tree *(green finger paint)*
    heart *(red or pink finger paint)*
    pumpkin *(orange finger paint)*
    leaves *(orange, yellow, red, brown, or green finger paint)*
    cross *(brown finger paint)*
    star *(yellow finger paint)*

    These shapes can be used as room decorations or for bulletin boards.
3. Make a wall mural with cutout shapes. Use flower shapes, stems, leaves, and butterflies. Put masking tape on the back of the pictures and arrange along the wall in a spring picture. Make a tall, slender wall mural in a narrow spot in the shape of a tree. Use brown pieces to form the trunk. Use a variety of fall leaf colors to make the top.

    Children will need to use different colors. They may write their names on the backs of the dried, finished mural before it is assembled.

Banners

Banners may be made from many materials. They can be made to hang from a nail or be taped on a wall or bulletin board. Banners generally have one to five words or one to two pictures on them. Banners may have many shapes.

Materials for backgrounds: felt, burlap, heavy cotton or sailcloth, paper

Banner lettering materials: felt, cotton or sailcloth, yarn, paper, colored string

Hanging banners need: yarn or string, and ¼″ dowel stick two inches wider than banner width

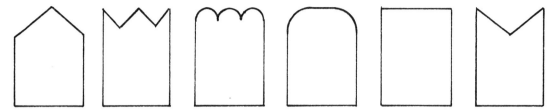

Some banner slogans: God Cares, One Way, His Is Love, Jesus Died for Me, I Am His Child, Jesus Loves Me, In His Spirit, King's Kid, Share His Love, Tell Others

Some banner shapes:

Paper banners: Use colored bulletin board paper, butcher paper, or construction paper. Can make letter, symbol, or picture shapes from tagboard. Children trace around tagboard shape on colored construction paper. Cut out. Glue to background.

To hang: Fold top down one inch over dowel on back. Glue edge. Hold until glue sets. Tie yarn to dowel on both sides of banner.

Felt banners: Will need sharp scissors to cut felt. Use tagboard patterns for letters, etc., as above. Use white or craft glue. May want to machine stitch flap for dowel hanger rather than gluing as with paper.

Burlap banners: May use cloth, felt, or paper letters and pictures on burlap. Trace and attach as above. May use yarn for stitching letters or stitching flap for hanging.

Pennants

Pennants are made in the same general way as banners. They are usually made of felt on felt. Slogans need to be three words or less, because pennants are smaller than banners. Pennants have two or three felt loops at the wide end. For waving, the loops may be glued around a ¼″ dowel stick fifteen to eighteen inches in length and attached to the back.

The loops may be 4″ by ½″ strips folded in half and attached to pennant back for fastening to a wall or bulletin board.

Watercolors

Children enjoy watercolors. Paints and brushes are inexpensive. It is best to use watercolors, however, after the children have used crayons, tempera paint, or other art mediums such as chalk. Older children have developed finer coordination more suited for the watercolor medium.

Watercolors have soft, pastel, somewhat translucent colors rather than the deep, rich coloring of temperas. Watercolors are used by lightly rubbing a damp brush over the color cake. Too much water runs the color cake into the color on either side in the pan. If the picture has been painted with lots of water, the paper may not lay flat when it dries. Too much water will also cause indistinct and smeary colors, and run lines if the picture is moved before it is completely dry.

Special watercolor paper works better than butcher paper or construction paper. Its surface isn't as porous, it is thicker, and pictures are more distinct.

Newspapers on the tables absorb any paint mess. Absorbent paper towels work well for cleaning brushes between colors and soaking up spills. Children need small dishes or jelly jars of water. Water needs to be changed as it muddies, or the colors will lose their clarity.

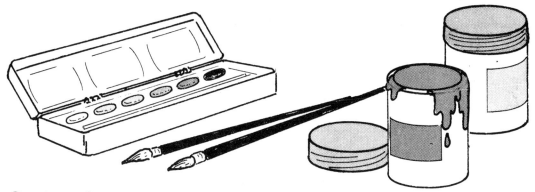

Cartooning

Cartooning means drawing a series of pictures, comic-strip fashion, in narrative sequence. The individual pictures may or may not contain captions of dialogue or explanation. Teacher may have paper prepared with cartoon like boxes already drawn or may use blank papers, normal size or smaller. The size of the cartoons desired will dictate the size of the box outline or piece of paper for each portion of the sequence. The pictures need not be elaborate. For younger children, simple stick-like figures are fine.

This story technique may be used to:
1. Review story theme.
2. Conclude with example of Christian behavior of a real-life situation in a cartoon strip setup.
3. Review sequence and meaning of quarter's lessons—if about one person or subject.

There are several ways to implement this project:
1. Each child may set up his own strip or sequence.
2. Group may work together, each child doing one section or picture.
3. Teacher may set up first pictures in sequence, leaving a blank or two for conclusion drawn and captioned by student.
4. Teacher may have all pictures in sequence with just the caption boxes left for student to fill in.

Mosaics

Mosaics are decorations, patterns, or pictures made by inlaying or over-laying small pieces of different colored materials. The materials used for mosaics can be paper, cloth, tile pieces, tissue paper, or masking tape.

Cut or tear mosaic material in little pieces. Use white or craft glue. Spread glue lightly, a small section at a time. Place pieces and press to paper.

Posters or pictures can be made with pieces of cloth or construction paper glued on construction paper.

Vases for tissue flowers or dried flowers can be made from small mouth pop bottles or different size jars. They may be covered with either tissue paper or masking tape. For tissue paper mosaic, follow above instructions. When entire bottle is covered, coat mosaic with thin layer of glue. If tissue flowers are made from one or two of the colors on the bottle, the effect is striking. For masking tape mosaic, tear off ¾″ pieces of tape. Stick to bottle. When surface is covered, rub brown shoe polish over tape pieces. Tie ribbon yarn around top of bottle. Fill with dried flowers or weeds.

Photography

Children enjoy looking at pictures of themselves and their friends over and over.

Bulletin boards make good display areas for photographs. Such a board will be enjoyed for several weeks. Photographs displayed may be taken of children participating in art projects, listening to stories, acting out lessons, playing games, singing, or other usual Sunday activities. Special field trips, award ceremonies, picnics, swimming parties, hikes, birthday parties, holiday get-togethers, and children's camp all provide excellent opportunities for posed and candid pictures.

Older children may enjoy taking some photographs. If they don't have cameras to use, the teacher may supervise the use of one.

Murals

A mural is a long picture, wall size or bulletin board size, drawn to illustrate a theme or story. It may be added to each Sunday for a few weeks or for a quarter.

A mural may be drawn free hand by the children. It may be lightly sketched in by adults and colored by younger children.

Many adults believe they could not draw a mural. An easy way to produce a mural is to copy the scene you wish to use on an overhead transparency. Place a blank transparency over the picture. Trace the picture. Then place the transparency on the projector. Project the picture onto a large piece of white butcher paper taped to a wall. Trace the picture in the size you wish. Size may be adjusted by moving the projector closer or farther away from the piece of paper.

A picture can also be enlarged using an opaque projector, or with a small plastic enlarger *(found in many mail order catalogs)*.

TV Box

The TV box is really a specialized mural.

The box and size of paper for the TV depend upon the size of pictures to be drawn.

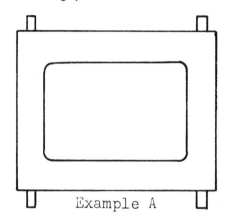

Example A

Cut a hole in the side of the box the size of the screen to be simulated. Leave at least a 3″ border or frame. Use two dowel sticks ¹/₃″ to ¹/₂″ in diameter for turning the pictures in sequence. In the top and bottom of the box, near the corners, cut small holes for each of the dowels. These holes should be hidden behind the frame around the screen. When the paper is attached to the dowels, they will stay in place. *(See example A.)*

Dowels may be positioned through the sides of the TV box rather than through the top and bottom. *(See example B.)* With top and bottom placement, pictures may be turned to follow the left/right reading pattern. With dowels in the side, the picture is turned frame by frame from top to bottom. Individual frame spots will have to be set up to move logically in the direction you choose to have dowels set.

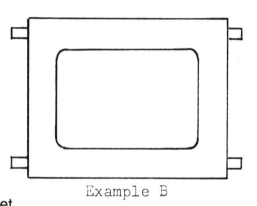

Example B

For the pictures, use butcher paper just a little wider than the screen opening. Unless the scene is to be one long continuous roll, a faint outline of the picture size should be drawn to show children frame placement for operating the production. Have a frame at the beginning for the title. Have a frame at the end for a Bible verse or two. The last frame could have "The End" written over it. Tape ends of roll to dowels in the box.

Children may narrate story and add music if they like as they turn dowels and move the story pictures along.

If the quarter's lessons follow one or two characters, this is a good activity for those who finish early. A scene or two can be added each week. When the quarter is finished, the TV box makes a good review for all the children.

Chalk or Pastels

This art medium is really called pastels. Pastels come in many sizes, shapes, and kinds. They range from small sets of sixteen or so colors, costing less than two dollars, to larger, more expensive sets. Some pastels are round, some square, some hexagonal. Some are covered with paper in crayon fashion. Some have oil mixed with the pastel to prevent smearing.

Remove paper from pastels. Break into several different sizes. When storing pastels, be certain to put each in the tray with its own color. Pastels rub off on each other easily.

For beginners, newsprint is good and inexpensive. As the student gains experience, or with older children, various colors of construction paper may be used for the background. When brushed over with a wet brush, colors can be blended and shaded.

Pad the worktables with several layers of newspaper. This serves two purposes. It provides table cover for easier cleanup, and a better picture can be created if the underlying surface has a little give.

Hold the pastel so it lays flat on the paper. Place it between the thumb and fingers so entire surface of pastel rubs on the page. Do not hold the pastel in a traditional pencil hold. Keep the arm *(from elbow to wrist)* up slightly so it doesn't rub across and smear the colors.

The different ways to draw with pastels are called strokes. The flat stroke leaves a solid shape like a rectangle. The edge stroke makes lines when the corner side of the pastel is used. The curved stroke makes an arc. Other strokes add shading and texture.

Pressure gives the pastels different color values. Value refers to the intensity or depth of color. Press harder, and get a darker value. Lighter strokes produce lighter colors. This is where the padding on the table really helps.

It takes practice, but applying color, discovering form, and experimenting can result in some interesting pictures. Pastels may be used as background pictures for dioramas, puppet shows, or as a project to add variety to the Sunday-school program.

Completed pictures or backgrounds may be sprayed with a fixative to keep them from smearing. Most hobby and craft stores carry such fixative.

Tempera Paint

Tempera paint is a powdered paint that usually comes in a shaker can. Its colors are opaque and brilliant. Tempera paint will dry and cake when exposed to air, so wash brushes out quickly. Keep lids tightly-closed on jars of mixed paint when not in use. Follow directions for mixing. Use large brushes.

Tempera is more effective for large pictures, easel style. It does not work as well for small, intricate pictures. It is suitable for painting large papier-mache projects. It may be used as part of other art projects—such as Blow Painting.

Newsprint or butcher paper is ideal for this work.

64

Blow Painting

Use a plastic straw, tempera paint, and construction paper.

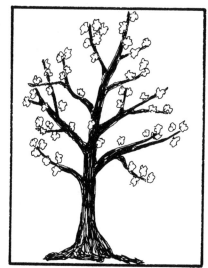

Dip straw into tempera paint. Hold finger on end of straw until it is positioned over where paint goes. Release finger and let paint drop onto paper. Blow through the straw, pushing the paint with the air.

Many designs and pictures may be made this way. Any color paint may be used with any color construction paper, as long as the colors contrast.

An especially pretty picture done in this way emphasizes the beauty of God's world. Use blow painting to make a tree or branch base on paper. Glue popcorn on the page to resemble trees in bloom. Blue construction paper, brown tempera paint, and white popcorn make a very attractive contrast.

Paper

Almost any kind of paper may be used for some kind of art project. Construction paper is an all-time favorite. Other papers or paper products which may be used are: butcher paper, tissue paper, facial tissue, old greeting cards, old coloring books, old magazines, tagboard, paper plates, paper cups, cupcake cups, and poster board.

Tagboard

Tagboard is heavy paper the color and weight of manila file folders. Office and school supply stores sell it in 9″ x 12″ or 12″ x 18″ sheets. Use old manila file folders if tagboard can't be found.

Storing Scissors

Scissors may be stored in small boxes and handed out when they are to be used. There are other ways, however, that also work.

One is to use colored Styrofoam egg cartons. Turn carton upside down. With a sharp knife, put a hole in each egg section. Slip a pair of scissors into the hole. If the Sunday-school department sits in small groups at individual tables when they do art work, use the six or eight pack carton available in some grocery stores, or fill the larger cartons half full.

Small boxes, just scissor size, may be decorated with contact paper or children's gift wrap paper. Each class, table, or group may have their own box decorated differently from the others.

Cutting Paper

Children enjoy cutting construction paper into shapes for projects. These projects may be simple cards, portions of story pictures, bulletin board borders or decorations, flowers, animals, special shapes to write Bible verses on, and countless other things.

If a fairly uniform shape is desired from or for each child, it may be helpful to have several tagboard patterns for children to trace around.

Preschool and kindergarten level coloring books have a variety of large person, place, thing, and seasonal pictures. To get picture shape on tagboard, lay carbon paper on the tagboard. Lay picture page over both and trace with heavy strokes. Then cut out the shape. Trace around it on other tagboard to make several patterns. It may be the actual picture in the coloring book can be colored, cut out, and used.

Teachers of very young children may wish to have items already traced, xeroxed, or dittoed on the paper to give them guidelines for cutting. Be certain to use large, uncomplicated shapes. Young children have not developed the eye/hand coordination and muscular control to cut out intricate patterns.

Many seasonal things may be cut out to decorate windows, walls, or other room areas. Some of the obvious ones are leaves, pumpkins, and turkeys for fall, snowflakes for winter, hearts for February, raindrops and flowers for April and May.

Children enjoy cutting paper strips to make paper chains for decorating Christmas trees, as bulletin board edges, or for decorating rooms for parties.

Tearing Paper

Construction paper torn in little pieces may be used to make mosaic-like pictures depicting Bible scenes, home scenes, or holiday scenes.

Cards used to spell out letters in songs may be constructed by tearing small pieces of paper, gluing them on a larger piece of construction paper in the shape of the letter desired. *(See Example A.)*

Posters with one word themes *(Example B)* or holiday shapes *(Example C)* may be done with torn pieces of paper.

Example A ''I Love Him Better Every Day''

Example B

Example C

Paper Sculpture

Folding, gluing, taping, or stapling paper to represent a real-life item falls in the category of paper sculpture.

Paper sculpture projects may be simple projects such as:

66

Crown—Cut out a crown shape. Fit to size of head. Staple or tape paper to hold that head size.

Lesson suggestions—Josiah, boy king. David. Any lesson dealing with a king

Trumpets—Fold and fasten paper in a cone or megaphone shape.

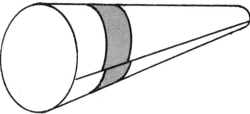

Lesson suggestions—Trumpet of the Lord calls Moses to Mount Sinai (Exodus 19:16)

—Lord instructs Moses in uses of trumpet (Numbers 10:2)

—Joshua and the battle of Jericho (Joshua 6:4)

—Trumpet sound—the end of the age (Revelation 8:6)

Scrolls—Use white piece of paper approximately 3 1/2" high and 8" wide. Glue or tape each end to a 4" dowel or popsicle stick. Roll each end toward the center.

Lesson suggestions—Any lesson teaching about God's Word in Hebrew form

—Stories of prophets writing down God's Word

—Hebrew boys learning Scripture (Paul, Timothy)

—History of the Bible

More complicated projects for older children may be:

Model Temple—Most Bible book and supply stores carry a punch out booklet model of the temple.

Model Village—Made by folding paper into house, tree, and wall shapes. Many public libraries have books about paper folding in their children's section. A village of Bible times could be made.

African Villages—A punch out booklet containing an African village sells in many stores carrying children's books. Use for an African missionary emphasis.

Other Paper Projects

Tri-folds

Tri-folds are made of large—medium to heavy weight construction paper. The two sides are folded in toward the middle so three sections are made. Proportions are usually equal thirds. Tops of the different portions may vary slightly in shape.

Tri-folds often represent different aspects of the same subject. Some examples:

- Seasonal changes in plants or animals
- Different life stages of some person *(baby Jesus, ministry, death on cross)*

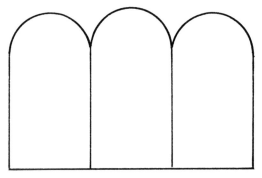

Story Parts:
1. Noah's ark *(building boat, rain, beneath rainbow)*
2. Moses *(mother makes basket, in reeds, princess finds)*

Daily Living Activity:
(morning, midday, evening)

(work, play, worship)

Booklets

Booklets are usable in a variety of ways.

Blank page booklets:
1. For field trip information
2. For lesson information or reveiw
3. For keeping a diary of:
    a. Daily activity
    b. Religious growth
    c. Personal experiences
4. For art related to lessons
5. For poetry or music

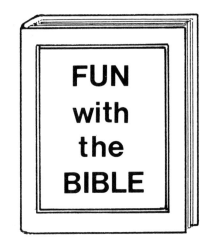

Puzzle Booklets

May hold a series of Bible verses in puzzle form. Puzzles are to be worked and verses memorized. Have a record keeping sheet in front. See Memory Work section for example.

Bible Memorization Booklets

These are set up with fill-in sentences and pictures. See section on Memory Work.

Booklet Covers

Make of construction paper, colored butcher paper, white or colored ditto or xerox paper. Covers can be decorated entirely by children or have duplicated, teacher-drawn pictures to color.

Bookmarks

Bookmarks may be made in several ways and of different types of paper.

Bookmarks can be sketched on ditto or xerox paper by teacher, cut out and colored by children.

They may be made of construction paper. Children color a picture on them or cut

out pictures to paste on.

Children enjoy painting and making them on watercolor paper.

Stitchery

Stitchery may be simple or complicated. Children as young as three or four can do some kinds of stitchery. Older children enjoy this art if it is presented in a way to spark their interest.

Young children like to use purchased thread-around-the-picture type cards. They can work on cloth or burlap if it is anchored by a hoop or frame. Teachers will need to show them how to thread the needle *(or thread it for them)* and make simple stitches.

Older children enjoy more challenging work. Make a stitch chart on cloth. Mount and label it. Samples of stitchery appropriate to children's ages should be shown. If real samples are available, use them. Otherwise, pictures will give children an idea and stimulate their own thinking.

Stitchery books show stitches and how to make them. They give helpful tips about threading needles, planning a design, using color, and work appropriate to a child's age. *(Show samples.)*

The public library will have books on stitchery in both the adult and children's sections.

Papier-Mache

Papier-mache projects have great versatility. They will take more than one Sunday, however. A project should be allowed two Sundays. One Sunday is for making the item. The week in between gives time for it to dry. The second Sunday may be used to decorate it.

Papier-mache may be used to make many items from puppet heads, masks, decorative boxes, animals, fruits, and sculptures to wall ornaments and landscape features for relief maps or dioramas.

The dictionary defines this French term, papier-mache, as literally meaning "chewed paper."

As has been mentioned before, care needs to be taken to protect tables and floors during this activity. A large piece of plastic on the floor under the table used for pasting will save messes on the carpet. The table should also be covered with plastic, oil cloth, or waxed butcher paper.

Ways to Use Papier-Mache

There are three basic ways to use the papier-mache technique. One uses torn paper strips *(long or short depending on the size of the project)* dipped in liquid adhesive. Another uses several layers of paper glued together to form a large sheet. When this sheet is dampened, it may be shaped over a base. The third method makes a paper mash which can be used like molding clay.

Paper

Almost any kind of paper may be used. The most popular is newspaper. However, kitchen towels, facial tissue, tissue paper, old magazines, and toilet paper will work.

Making Liquid Adhesive

Several kinds of paste or glue may be used. Wheat paste mixed to a tomato soup consistency works well. Water may need to be added as paste thickens. Nontoxic wallpaper paste may be used, basically in the same way as wheat paste. White all-purpose glue may be diluted with water—using half glue to half water.

Applying Liquid Adhesive

Dipping—When dipping paper strips into paste mixture, be certain not to saturate the paper. Only enough adhesive is necessary to make paper strips stick together. Too much adhesive adds more water than necessary and slows the drying process. It may be helpful to hold the strip in one hand and wipe between fingers of the other hand to strip off excess paste.

Brush—Using brush, apply paste to paper strip. Do not saturate paper. Be certain edges receive paste mixture.

Applying Paper Strips

Torn paper edges blend into the project better than cut edges.

Newspaper may be torn using a yardstick. Lay yardstick on paper three or four single sheets thick. Press yardstick down firmly, leaving an inch of paper showing. Tear along edge of yardstick.

As each strip is applied, and pressed on firmly, all wrinkles should be smoothed away. Each strip should slightly overlap the previous one.

Each layer of paper should lay in a different direction to give strength to the finished product. By alternating paper colors for each layer, it is easier for children to see when they have completed an overall layer. If using newspaper, alternate black and white layers with colored ads or comic section layers.

Items to Use for Base

Papier-mache may be applied over almost any kind of base. Balloons make good oval shape bases. Aluminum foil can be formed into almost any shape and layered over. Crushed and tied newspaper, rolled and taped newspaper, clay, cans, cardboard boxes *(large or small,)* Styrofoam, plastic jars or bottles, paper tubes, and chicken wire may be some items for bases. Small cans, parts of egg cartons, etc. may be taped *(masking tape)* onto base to form arms, legs, or interesting shapes.

When making masks, form the base *(clay or newspaper)* and then lay waxed paper over it. When mask is dry, lift away from base.

Pulp of Mash Papier-Mache

Some hobby stores or art supply stores sell prepared mash *(Celluclay)* or can order it.

Mash may be made of any cardboard pressed product like egg cartons, paper tubes, or paper dividers. Toilet paper, kitchen paper towels, facial tissue, newspaper, or regular school newsprint paper may be used.

To make mash, soak pieces of paper in diluted glue or wheat paste mixture for approximately eight hours. When it seems to be a pulpy mess, squeeze liquid out. Use as modeling clay.

Mash may be used over a base or by itself to form shapes.

Tips for Drying

As papier-mache strips are worked, wipe off extra glue. Make certain strips are damp enough to adhere, but not so damp they will slow the drying process.

Projects should dry in thirty-six to fifty-six hours unless the air is very damp. If projects are not drying fast enough, put them in a warm, sunny place or set in a low temperature oven *(150°)* with door cracked open *(to allow moisture to escape)* until project is dry.

Decorating the Project

If finished item is less smooth than desired, sand rough edges or bump spots.

Projects may be painted with tempera paints or water base acrylic paints. When paint has dried, item may be sprayed with a fixative.

Small pictures, yarn, felt, beads, sequins, buttons, or other decorative bits may be glued onto the surface.

Plaster of Paris

This white, flour-like powder turns into a paste which hardens in a few minutes when mixed with water. It is poured into a mold, allowed to set, removed, and decorated when dry.

Plaster of paris may be used for entire plaques, letters or figures for plaques, figures for dioramas and displays, jewelry, fruit, vegetables, religious artifacts, animals, and many other projects.

Molds

Most molds now are made of white plastic. Older molds were made of rubber-like material which peeled off dried figures.

Molds may be purchased in many art, hobby, craft, or discount stores.

Mixing Plaster of Paris

General directions usually advise mixing one part water to two parts plaster. It should look like runny pancake batter.

When mixing, stir only until lumps are dissolved. Too much stirring hastens the setting process. The plaster may set up before it is all poured into the mold.

It is better to mix small amounts *(one to two cups)* if small, individual pieces are being poured. The plaster sets up very quickly. It is advisable to mix a lot only if one bigger project is being poured.

Not enough water—plaster will set up while being stirred to remove lumps.

Too much water—the top of the mold will have water on it after plaster has been poured. If too wet, it may need to be washed out and repoured in order to set correctly.

Using Molds

When using plastic molds, spray the mold with some type of unfloured, vegetable pan spray. This helps in the removal of the figure.

Plaster will set up in an hour or so, but it may be too green to remove without breaking the item. It is best to let it set for several hours or overnight. A large item should dry longer.

Decorating

When plaster of paris items have dried for twelve to twenty-four hours, or dried sufficiently to be light, look white, and not break apart when removed from the mold, paint the item. Tempera or water base acrylic paints work well. When sprayed with a fixative, they have gloss and a richer color tone.

Age of Children

The age of the children doing the project will determine how much they will be able to help in the actual mixing and pouring process. It will also determine the type of project attempted. Younger children should not be given complicated figures with small features to paint.

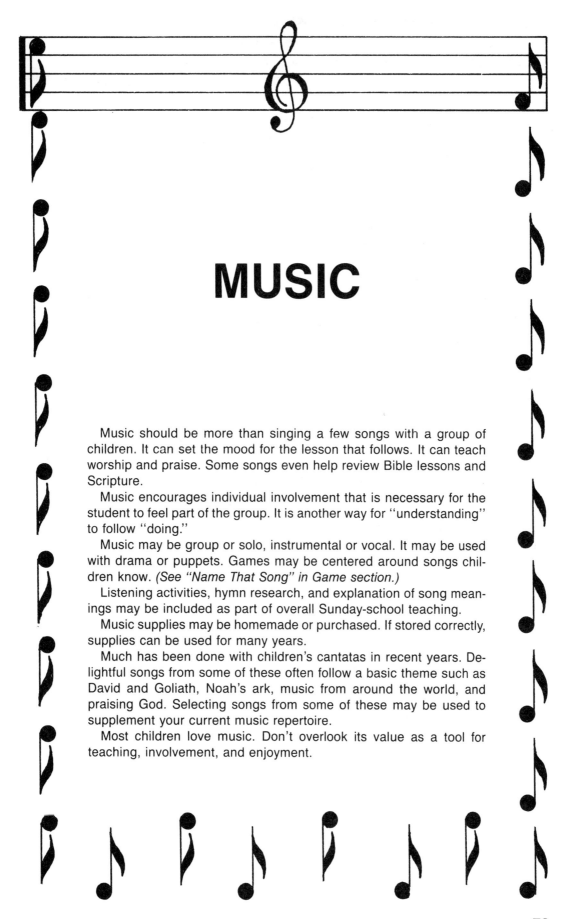

MUSIC

Music should be more than singing a few songs with a group of children. It can set the mood for the lesson that follows. It can teach worship and praise. Some songs even help review Bible lessons and Scripture.

Music encourages individual involvement that is necessary for the student to feel part of the group. It is another way for "understanding" to follow "doing."

Music may be group or solo, instrumental or vocal. It may be used with drama or puppets. Games may be centered around songs children know. *(See "Name That Song" in Game section.)*

Listening activities, hymn research, and explanation of song meanings may be included as part of overall Sunday-school teaching.

Music supplies may be homemade or purchased. If stored correctly, supplies can be used for many years.

Much has been done with children's cantatas in recent years. Delightful songs from some of these often follow a basic theme such as David and Goliath, Noah's ark, music from around the world, and praising God. Selecting songs from some of these may be used to supplement your current music repertoire.

Most children love music. Don't overlook its value as a tool for teaching, involvement, and enjoyment.

Accompaniment Instruments

The piano is possibly the all-time favorite for the accompaniment of vocal music.

However, variety adds interest and zest. If someone in the church plays guitar, have them come in occasionally. If no one plays an instrument, or if you can't get an accompanist, use children's records or tapes and sing along.

Try using a tape recorder to tape one or two verses of a round, then play it while the group sings the second round part with themselves. Older children may want to sing two parts of the round along with the prerecorded first part to make a three part round.

The autoharp makes an additional change. With some help, children can play this instrument rather quickly.

The Autoharp and Children

Cut a piece of paper to fit under the strings on the left side of the autoharp. On that paper, type a simple song the children know well. Choose one that does not use more than two or three chords. Write above the words where chords change. Children strum the autoharp and press chord buttons indicated. A sample diagram is shown below. Also given is a well-known children's chorus with sample chords.

If you do not feel capable of chording songs your group knows, ask the help of someone who plays guitar or piano. Just be certain to have the autoharp with you, because it does not have all the chords available to guitar and piano. Many children's songbooks now have guitar chords written above the music. These work well for the autoharp, too.

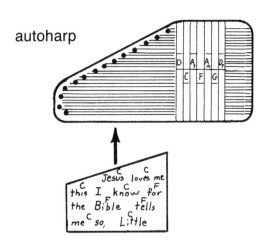

autoharp

Jesus Loves Me

```
  C     C       C    C
Jesus loves me! this I know,
  F       F    F        C
For the Bible tells me so;
  C    C      C     C
Little ones to Him belong;
  F       C      G       C
They are weak but He is strong.
  C    C    F    F
Yes, Jesus loves me!
  C    C    G    G
Yes, Jesus loves me!
  C    C    F    F
Yes, Jesus loves me.
     C    G     C
The Bible tells me so.
```

Sample copy of music to be slipped under autoharp wires. Tape bottom edge of music paper to lower edge of autoharp at arrow point.

Music Supplies

Purchased Song Cards

Many attractive song cards can be purchased from religious supply stores. Usually there are two copies of the song included loose in the packaging.

Music Notebook

Compiling a music notebook offers several advantages. It provides a central, organized music book for your department. It prevents losing half-page sheets which come with purchased song cards. Songs from other books may be pulled and placed in the notebook. This eliminates flipping through several books each Sunday morning.

Use a loose-leaf notebook with 8½″ x 11″ blank pages. Glue (*rubber cement works best*) the music to the blank page. Keep an index in front. Make a note on the bottom of each page for the source of the song, and any visual aids that go with it. If a key change has been made to accommodate guitar or autoharp accompaniment, make a note at the top.

Store notebook with music cards and supplies.

Homemade Song Cards

If you choose to make your own cards to add variety and save money, consider some of these suggestions.

1. Use a variety of light colored poster board.
2. Use manuscript letters for song words. Children and teachers can read them easily from anywhere in the room.
3. Poster board may be cut into shapes. A song about a butterfly may be cut into a butterfly shape. Don't make shapes too complicated for the board is not really easy to cut.

4. Old teacher's packet pictures may be used to decorate the songs. For instance, a song about Jesus loving all children may use missionary pictures of children from other lands. Any song about Jesus could have a picture of Jesus glued on it.
5. Pictures may be drawn along the top or bottom with art pencils.
6. If picture cards or picture sticks are used by children during the song, glue an example on the master song card. If a dowel stick is used on the card, a hot glue gun or carpenter's glue may attach it more securely.
7. Songs may be made in rebus form. A rebus has some pictures substituted for words. The song may be written as usual, except have small pictures in places of words such as Bible, hand, etc.

Storing Song Cards

Purchased cards are usually smaller than homemade cards, and are designed to be held by teachers or children.

Homemade song cards may be hung by two or three large metal rings from a specially built rack. *(See Example A.)* They may be propped on an easel or chart rack. *(See Example B.)* They may be pinned or fastened *(with large clipboard metal clips)* to a central bulletin board. *(See Example C.)* Children may enjoy holding some of these, too.

Know the songs well enough to look at the children while singing. They watch the leader as they sing. Smiles and some facial expression from the song leader increase student participation and enjoyment.

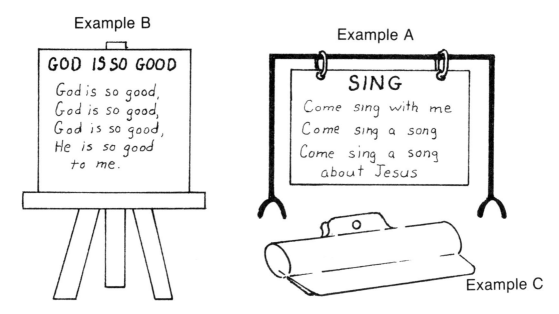

Example B

GOD IS SO GOOD

God is so good,
God is so good,
God is so good,
He is so good
to me.

Example A

SING

Come sing with me
Come sing a song
Come sing a song
about Jesus

Example C

Storing Supplies

Song cards, purchased or homemade, should be stored flat or standing up in a place where their corners and pictures will be protected. Song charts fastened to a rack store well in that form, if protected from excessive moving about. Easels and charts store well behind pianos or in closets.

Small picture cards or sticks may be stored in appropriately sized boxes or in ziplock plastic bags. Ziplock bags can have a hole punched in corner and be hung, or they can be laid flat in a box or on a shelf.

Singing

Singing songs and choruses is made more personal and exciting by using hand or body motions. Many children's songs lend themselves to this.

Emphasize particular parts of song lyrics by using picture cards or pictures glued on sticks. When the lyrics are sung, the child raises or waves a card or stick picture in the appropriate place.

Pictures can be cut from magazines and glued to cards or sticks. Old Sunday-school student booklets, take-home papers, or teacher's packets supply such pictures. Pictures colored and cut from children's coloring books, or those found in inexpensive children's books, are possibilities also.

The cards can be construction paper or colored tagboard cut to the shape of the item—such as sun, bell, angel, and so forth.

Dowel sticks, tongue depressors, or popsicle sticks make good handles for lyric cards.

Lyric Cards or Sticks

Following are some suggestions for lyric cards or sticks.

rocks	trees	flowers	mountains	the seasons
sun	moon	stars	rivers	ocean
sheep	fish	lions	birds	other animals
hands	eyes	feet	noses	praying hands
ears	mouths	hearts	frowns	smiling faces
children	parents	friends	go signs	stop signs
roads	bridges	lights	doors	church
home	school	Bible	cross	crown
bells	angels	heaven	manger	baby Jesus
food	fruit	vegetables	shoes	clothing
clock	globe	money		

individual letters for spelled out words (B-I-B-L-E)

Rhythms

Rhythms may be as simple as a particular clapping pattern in a song.
Percussion

One way to enjoy rhythm is to use the body in making percussion sounds. The main ways to use the body as a percussion instrument are: clapping, leg slapping, finger snapping, foot stamping, and tongue clicking.

Some of these body sounds may already be included in songs you know. If not, add them to an appropriate song. Contests may be held between boys and girls to enliven the music. The fun thing about this is that it needs no special equipment because children have their own.

Rhythm Bands

It is a rare young child who does not enjoy taking part in a rhythm band. If purchasing instruments is a problem, try some of the following ideas for homemade instruments. If you can add a triangle or two, and a few other instruments, all to the good.

Children may even be able to help make some of these instruments.
Wood Blocks

Scrap two by fours, cut in various sizes, give different tones. Wooden dowels or different sized wooden spoons also change pitch.
Spoon Clappers

Metal spoons are clapped together, back to back, by being held between the fingers of one hand or being clapped together using two hands.

Drums

Childrens' play drums may be used. Coffee cans and tea cans with plastic lids make good drums. Empty plastic gallon jugs, lids on, turned upside down work well. Old oatmeal boxes or empty salt boxes can be used. Children may use wooden dowels, wooden spoons, or their hands to produce sound.

Jingle Bells

Fabric bands sewn in a circle, sized to slip over a child's fingers and fit into the palm of his hand, can have two or three bells attached. When the band is on the hand, the bells should be on the back of the palm. When child shakes his hand, bells jingle.

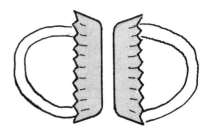

Tambourine

Staple or tape two foil pie pans together, after putting a few dried beans or bottle caps inside. Children may shake or tap the tambourine against their hand.

Castanets

May be made from metal bottle caps. Finger-sized loops of felt, elastic, or cloth may be glued to the inner side of the bottle cap. *(Hot glue holds especially well, but other glues will hold for a while.)* Child slips one cap on thumb and other on middle finger and taps them together.

Triangles

.These may be purchased or ordered from instrumental music stores. An old coat hanger, tapped with a nail, will substitute but does not have the same ring.

Kazoos

Comb Kazoo—Use a small man's comb. Fold a piece of wax paper in half. Slip comb into fold, pointing teeth into fold. Child hums melody while holding comb and paper to lips.

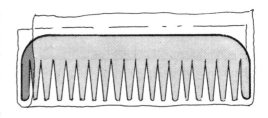

Paper Tube Kazoo—Toilet paper tube or ½" kitchen towel tube is a good size. Cut piece of wax paper 6" x 6". Fold the wax paper loosely around end of tube, fastening with a loose rubber band. Folding the paper tightly or using too tight a rubber band does not allow enough air

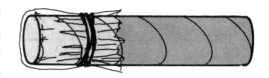

to circulate to cause vibrations when child hums loudly into the open end. Put tube right over mouth.

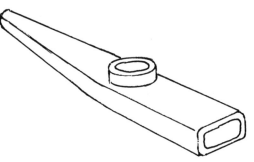

Plastic Kazoo—These are not too expensive and would be a popular addition to the band instruments.

Sand Blocks

Cover two small wooden blocks with medium to finely grained sand paper. The paper may be glued, stapled, or tacked on. Children use by rubbing blocks back and forth over each other.

Scrapers

Use a wooden dowel or spoon and run it down the side of a cheese or vegetable grater.

Washboard

Same principle as scraper. Children love to use old washboards as part of a rhythm band *(if you can find anyone willing to part with one).* With the renewed interest in antiques, it might be possible to find a reproduction washboard at a reasonable price.

Rattles

Pop cans, filled with a few dried beans and taped shut *(masking tape),* make excellent rattles. Children may decorate construction paper, wrap around can, and tape. Small jelly jars with metal lids, baby food jars with lids, or cans with plastic lids can be used for rattles when filled with a few beans.

Cymbals

Old pan lids of an approximate size can be clanged together as cymbals. A cheaply purchased child's set is very popular also.

Bells

Any size small metal or Christmas type bell may be used.

Tone Bottles

Fill old glass pop bottles with different levels of water. The bottle openings are blown into to produce a tone. Bottles may also be tapped with a stick.

Rhythm Sticks, Claves

Rhythm sticks may be wooden dowels approximately ½″ thick and 13″ to 15″ long. These are tapped against each other. Child holds one in each hand.

Claves are shorter (5″ to 6″) thick (1″) dowel-like pieces of hardwood. One piece is held lightly between fingers and pad just below thumb. The other is tapped on the one held in the fingers. Holding the clave too tightly mutes the tone.

Maracas

Anything hollow, round, or slightly larger than an average fist can serve as a maraca. Put a few beans in it and attach it to a stick for shaking.

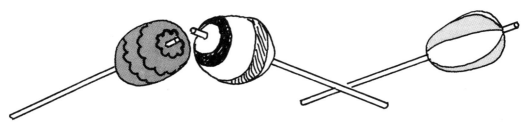

Drill a small hole in dried gourds. Glue or tape a dowel or stick in the gourd. Shake. The dried seeds already in the gourd will make a soft, maraca sound.

You may papier-mache over small balloons. *(See Art section relating to papier-mache.)* Be certain several layers are used around the balloon so it will stand up to use as a maraca. When dry, pop balloon. If necessary, make a small hole in the little end of the balloon shape. Insert a few beans or dried seeds. Tape or glue a wooden dowel in the small hole. Children may wish to paint or decorate maracas and maraca sticks.

Collecting Rhythm Instruments

Let your search for rhythm instruments be known among friends and church members. It is amazing how many items people have in their homes. People may even be willing to donate some rhythm instruments, materials for their making, or money to help purchase them.

Using Rhythm Instruments

Following are some ideas which may make rhythm band experiences more successful.

1. Children will enjoy band more if they get to take turns with the more popular instruments—kazoo, triangles, bells, and cymbals.
2. If children can't seem to play and sing the music at the same time, tape the music or have someone play it on the piano. Little children get so involved in playing the instrument they often forget to sing.
3. Rhythm instruments are usually played to mark the beat of the song. They may be played with the melody as a change, or use special rhythms for special types of music—some Spanish songs and calypso Christmas songs.
4. Someone needs to conduct the band. Conductor stands in front of the children clapping his hands to indicate beat, or tapping two rhythm sticks together. Practice any special rhythms to be used with older children enough times for them to become proficient.
5. Conductor may wish to explain time signature in music (3/4, 4/4, 6/8, etc.) to older children.
6. Different instruments may be played during different parts of the song to add variety. It is better to have several instruments play together for a fuller sound. If the band has eight or ten instrument types, divide into two or three groups. If the song mentions just one sound—such as bells—try playing just that instrument for that phrase.
7. Experiment with a variety of sounds. Enjoy.

Performance Instruments

If we begin performing in public as a youngster, we often have more confidence in performing as an adult.

Occasionally there are children taking piano lessons or playing in fifth, sixth, or junior high bands. Encourage these children to play as part of a Sunday-school opening or special music time.

Parents who are paying for and encouraging their children in private lessons are usually very happy to have their children perform. Contact them three or four weeks ahead of the projected performance date.

Children who are afraid to play for the entire church might be willing to play for their own class. Beginners need to start in a less threatening environment.

Using your talents, serving God with what abilities you have, and developing new talents are part of some Sunday-school lessons. They provide excellent opportunities for children to perform.

Vocal Performance

Many children have very nice singing voices. Encourage them to sing solos, duets *(both children singing melody if they are young),* and in groups.

You may wish to work with the duet or group for a couple of Sundays in advance. Contact parents for suggestions and help as you did with instrumental solos.

Music With Puppets

Puppets and music work well together.

Using pictures and stick puppets with song portions has already been discussed. Another way is to use puppets to mime singing actually being done by children.

Puppet choirs can be organized. Children may furnish the music, or work the puppets to records or taped music.

Plan music to enhance a puppet performance—as introduction and closing elements.

Music With Drama

In the same way music enriches puppet shows, it may add to drama. Children can provide their own music or may select appropriate music for the story being dramatized.

Music Selection

Classical, country, religious, popular, and children's music offer a wide choice for Sunday-school use.

Children should be taught to choose their leisure listening music as carefully as they would chose their reading and viewing matter. When teaching this concept, small portions of carefully chosen drug and sex-related rock and some country music make good negative examples. Upper elementary age children are exposed to non-Christian ideas in some music they hear. Good teaching makes a difference.

Bible Review and Music

Many songs follow a Bible story line. These can be used with the lesson about which it teaches. The melody may be used in a music game to remind children of the lesson truth. There are many such songs. A few are listed here.

Little David Play on Your Harp
Only a Boy Named David
Zacchaeus Was a Wee Little Man
How Did Moses Cross the Red Sea?
The Wise Man and the Foolish Man
Songs about Noah's Ark *(from children's cantatas)*
Dare to Be a Daniel
Go Down Moses
We Are Climbing Jacob's Ladder
The Lord Is My Shepherd
The Good Shepherd
The Creation
This Little Light of Mine
For God So Loved the World
Peter, James, and John in a Sailboat
Silver and Gold Have I None
The Battle of Jericho
There Were Twelve Disciples
Fishers of Men

DRAMA

Children delight
in being part of
dramatic situations.
Drama need not be
complicated scripts, elaborate
costumes, or adult performances.
Drama can be used to review lessons, to present full lessons, and to
enrich lesson portions. It can be hand in glove with art and music,
using all three aspects to reinforce Bible truths. Children remember
what they *do* much longer than what they *hear.*

Types of Drama

Informal Drama

Informal drama is drama without a set dialogue or script. It can be used with a few children in front of the class, or with the whole class participating. It doesn't require experience or detailed production.

Informal drama can be a lesson review—acting out the story told that morning, with one child narrating the story line.

It can be children participating in parts of the story as the teacher tells it and directs them in what to do.

It can be an adult, dressed as one of the characters in the story, narrating and explaining events as he saw them.

Examples:

The Lost Sheep

Children make lamb puppets during presession activity. These can be simple paper bag puppets. As the teacher tells the story, children crawl around making lamb sounds and working their puppets. One child can be the lost sheep in a far corner of the room. Chairs may be used as an imaginary sheepfold. Shepherd pretends to look all over for the crying lamb until it is found. Children like to repeat this, taking turns being lamb and shepherd.

This drama may be done without puppets.

Daniel in the Lion's Den

Children make lion faces or masks as presession activity. When Daniel *(one child)* is thrown into the lion's den *(a circle of chairs),* all the children walk around him wearing lion masks and roaring. Other children may play parts of the king and the wicked men.

Drama may be done without masks or any special costuming.

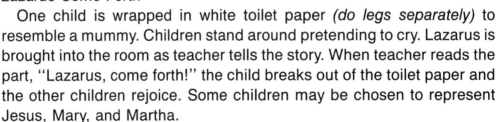

Lazarus Come Forth

One child is wrapped in white toilet paper *(do legs separately)* to resemble a mummy. Children stand around pretending to cry. Lazarus is brought into the room as teacher tells the story. When teacher reads the part, "Lazarus, come forth!" the child breaks out of the toilet paper and the other children rejoice. Some children may be chosen to represent Jesus, Mary, and Martha.

Costumes may or may not be used—as you wish.

Stoning of Stephen (or) *Stoning of Paul*

Children make rocks by crushing old newspapers into ball shapes.

This can be done in presession activity time without telling the children what it is for. A child is asked to represent Stephen, another to represent Paul. Children walk by Paul, giving him their coats or sweaters to hold. Then they throw the paper rocks and yell such things as, "Death to the Christians!"

The same basic drama can be used with modifications for the stoning of Paul.

Role Playing

Role playing is acting out a story and speaking the words of the characters. It usually is done without a script—children making up the dialogue.

Role playing helps children review the story, think more specifically about the story message, and feel something of what the Bible characters must have felt.

Story suggestions for role playing:

Good Samaritan (Luke 10:25-37)
Prodigal Son (Luke 15:11-32)
David and Goliath (1 Samuel 17)
Battle of Jericho (Joshua 6)
Selling of Joesph (Genesis 37:12-28)
Calling of Samuel (1 Samuel 3:1-18)
Calling of Saul (Acts 9:1-18)
Ruth and Naomi (Ruth 1:3-17)
Paul and Silas in Prison (Acts 16:16-34)

There are many other Bible stories which may be used for role playing.

Pantomime

This form of drama can be done without speaking. It may be done in a very stylized version or in simply acting out a role without talking. Pantomime may also be done while a record or tape-recorded story plays.

Radio or Television Program

This form of drama is a good way for children to learn about radio and television work—and how to use it to share about Jesus.

If it is possible, coordinate this drama form with a field trip to a local radio or television station.

When children have decided whether to do a radio or television broadcast, help them plan the elements of the program: Scripture, music, announcements, and message. Visual aids, skits, puppet plays, or drama could be used for the program.

The artwork, pretend microphones, etc. may be produced during presession or art activity time.

When program is complete and presentable, invite another Sunday-school group to view the finished product.

Tableau

Children decide on story and make a living picture of it—such as the manger scene.

Costumes

Costumes can be made from many things. They can be as simple as a mask or as complicated as a full costume with headgear.

Old sheets work well, using a basic pattern. *(See examples.)* Many parents are glad to send old sheets or towels to be cut up and used for costumes. The sheets can be dyed different colors before or after they are made into costumes.

Many fabric stores have sales of very cheap material. Fake gold and silver chain is sold in fabric stores by the yard for a small price. These chains make good necklaces for kings or other costumes.

A costume might consist of just a mask, a hat, or perhaps a paper cape. Masks may be made from paper plates, construction paper, or cloth and felt—with yarn, buttons, etc. added for special effects.

Costumes made of old sheets, with accessories, store easily in a box or drawer. Change them slightly and use them over and over for a variety of lessons.

Old robes, men's old shirts, old blouses, aprons, and other clothing items become costume parts. People are very good about donating old clothing or other costume materials if they know you need them.

A large grocery bag becomes many costumes. Cut a hole in the end for the head, and cut armholes in the sides. If fringed, the bag becomes an Indian outfit. The possibilities are endless. Paper bags also become head masks. Cut out eyes and mouth. Add ears, hair, and other features.

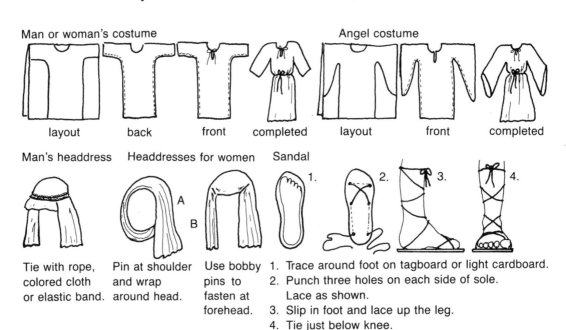

Man or woman's costume   Angel costume

layout   back   front   completed   layout   front   completed

Man's headdress   Headdresses for women   Sandal

Tie with rope, colored cloth or elastic band.

Pin at shoulder and wrap around head.

Use bobby pins to fasten at forehead.

1. Trace around foot on tagboard or light cardboard.
2. Punch three holes on each side of sole. Lace as shown.
3. Slip in foot and lace up the leg.
4. Tie just below knee.

PUPPETS

Using puppets sometimes seems like a lot of work for a limited-use item—at least in relation to Sunday school.

Puppets, however, can add a great deal more variety than just the occasional lesson written as a puppet play—when presented with music and scenery.

Try using puppets in some of the following ways:

• As a craft item children make to use later in acting out a lesson
• As the speaker for opening exercises or announcements
• As host or hostess to greet visitors
• As a puppet choir—alternating song parts
• As stick puppet parts to illustrate song parts
• As a way to review Bible lessons
• As a special character designed to help announce birthdays.

Younger children—fourth grade and down—love puppets. Occasionally even older children enjoy their use.

The more actively involved a child becomes, the more learning he will retain. A child will remember more of Bible truth being discovered if he makes a simple paper puppet and takes part in the lesson. If he sits passively and watches a more professional performance done by adults, he will retain much less.

Explore the possibilities of using puppets now and then for different aspects of the Sunday-school hour—welcoming, birthdays, announcements, taking offering, giving instructions, teaching games, as well as teaching lessons.

A puppet or two can become another part of the Sunday-school teacher's permanent supplies to use over and over again in dozens of ways.

Kinds of Puppets

Puppets can represent people, talking animals and plants, or talking inanimate things such as stars, rocks, houses, sun, etc.

Puppets can be made of almost anything. Following is a list of types of puppets:

- paper bag puppets (A)
- paper plate puppets (B)
- paper tube puppets (C)
- detergent bottle puppets (D)
- box puppets
- chenille wire puppets
- popsickle stick puppets (E)
- rod or dowel stick puppets
- clothespin puppets (F)
- sock puppets (G)
- wooden spoon puppets (H)
- construction paper puppets (E)
- cloth and Styrofoam ball puppets (I)
- magazine picture puppets
- finger puppets (J)
- puppet drawn on hand puppets (K)
- string puppets—marionettes
- dressed cloth puppets

Scraps of almost everything can be used to make puppets. Teachers can keep a bag handy at home to toss in all kinds of odds and ends—from craft, cooking, and sewing activities. These can be stored in a bigger box at church to be used by children making puppets.

Turn Sunday-School Lesson Into Puppet Script

1. Focus on the one main Bible truth you wish to teach—make it simple.
2. Make a list of characters needed. It's better not to have more than three or four—gets too complicated, and it puts too many people in a small area trying to work at once.
3. Change story to dialogue. Keep speaking parts as short as possible. Make special notes by the speaking parts if the puppeteers are to use special actions or props.
4. Keep the story simple—focus on main events. Have a definite beginning, middle, and ending.
5. Have puppets use lots of action.
6. Set an atmosphere or mood for the play.
7. Stage may be:
   (a) Table turned on its side—puppeteers behind.
   (b) Piano draped with a sheet—puppeteers behind.
   (c) Two or three chairs with backs to children and draped with a sheet—puppeteers behind.
   (d) Room divider—puppeteers behind.
   (e) Large box with window cut out—puppeteers inside.
   (f) More professional puppet play frame draped with curtains.
   If using scenery, describe settings or backdrops. The making of the settings or backdrops may be part of the craft or art time in Sunday school.
8. Itemize all props or special effects you might need.
9. After play is adapted from story, read and tape record it to play back for evaluation and change.
10. If you wish, record the whole play on tape before the performance. Special sound effects as well as opening and closing music are included in this way. All concentration goes into puppet movement rather than parts and sounds. The end product is smoother and more believable to children.

There are many excellent books about puppets in print.

CREATIVE WRITING

Creative writing provides a much needed student response in communicating what he has learned and how he feels. It is another opportunity for student involvement in the learning process. It can be exciting and fun or serious and thoughtful, but it is important.

Much is done for children in our culture. This is evident in religious education, too. Publishers strive to provide the finest lesson materials available. Teachers train and study. They plan interest catching and holding activities. They teach and entertain.

Is it enough, however?

We hear in news reports across the country of concern over lowered student performance in academics. We hear of passive learners who have lost their creative ability.

A Sunday-school teacher's goal is to lead children to the Lord and to challenge them to reach out to others with the gospel. A child who cannot communicate his faith will be handicapped in leading others to God, perhaps into adulthood.

Creative writing can open the door to written and verbal communications skills.

A very large bonus in the process of communication becomes evident when the teacher listens to the children's ideas. We talk to, at, and with children, but how much do we *listen?* Confusion, incorrect information, and knowledge of the child's life and needs surface in conversations and written expression.

The projects need not be big or time-consuming. They can be adapted to the ability and interest of the age level. If planned to fit into the lesson theme, or to be a natural outgrowth of it, such writing projects extend learning. Tie them into art, drama, or community service projects for a multifaceted approach.

You may be pleased to discover creative writing a delight rather than a chore. Try some of the following suggestions or use them to trigger your own ideas.

Yes, Yes, Yes

Does creative writing sound like a lot of work? Do you think it might be difficult to motivate children to write creatively? Have past writing projects seemed like time-filling activities? Are your answers to these questions, yes, yes, yes? The following suggestions may open new doors for learning and reinforcing Bible information and application.

Anything which may be spoken may also be written on paper. Children's writing need not be formal or overly meticulous. Writing can be done with the entire class creating one composition together *(moderated by teacher),* in small groups, or as an individual activity.

As soon as children can draw a recognizable picture, they can participate in creative writing. This is done with a technique called "dictation." Children draw on the upper two-thirds or so of the paper. They "dictate" or tell the teacher what they wish printed under their picture.

Older children enjoy creative writing if it is presented in an interesting fashion. For instance, if written work is to be displayed on a bulletin board, to spark interest prepare the bulletin board background, lettering, and special effects before the writing project begins.

General Tips

Word bank • If all writing is about one basic subject, before writing begins, work with the children to compile a high-frequency list of words which might be used in the stories. Being unable to spell necessary words slows and discourages students. Post the word list on a chalkboard. Add other words as they are requested.

Ability levels • Children have different ability levels even in the same grade. Make allowances for the child whose reading skills are poor by letting him illustrate the story. A child may need to dictate his story to the teacher or a more capable child. Above all, praise children for the work they do, the creativity they show, and the effort they make. In creative writing, the teacher should place emphasis on ideas as well as on perfectly executed penmanship, punctuation, and spelling.

Motivate beginnings • Some children need to be motivated with thought-provoking questions or lead-in sentences. Examples of such questions are: What happened first? Why did that happen? What does that Bible verse mean? How did the Bible story end? Why did it end that way? Other lead-in suggestions are given under the short stories section.

Creative Writing Projects

Letter Writing
- to missionaries
- to a sick or absent friend
- thank you to pastor or teacher
- special notes and cards to parents

Plays
- simple scripts for puppet plays
- simple scripts for dramatizations

Newspapers
- see the bulletin board section

Short Stories
- modern day examples of Bible situations
- stories to illustrate "What if?"

Give open-ended sticky situations relating to real-life experiences children may have such as:

(1) What if you are in a store with friends and see them shoplift? What will you do?

(2) What if you are with friends and they begin taking drugs? What if they urge you to try drugs, too?

(3) What if you accidentally break something your mother really likes? You know she will be angry. How will you handle the situation?

(4) What if your best friend signals for you to show him/her your science test? You know he/she is close to failing and this test might make the difference. You are sitting next to each other, and maybe no one will ever know if you let him/her look. What will you do? Why?

- sharing a personal experience
- sharing plans for the future—college, occupation, travel, etc.

Descriptions
- seasonal, describing God's world *(perhaps accompanied by a picture)*
- describing a particular item from God's creation *(a leaf, a flower, a tree, a special pet or animal, a beautiful scenic or vacation spot, etc.)* See "Word Painting" in the bulletin board section.

Games

"Who Am I?"—Children prepare questions of varying difficulty for each Bible character assigned or studied. When game begins, children ask the most difficult questions first, easiest question last. Other children try to guess the Bible person's identity from the questions asked. Child with most correct answers wins.

"What Am I?"—Same procedure as for "Who Am I?" Questions will be written and asked about items from parables, Bible events associated with a specific thing, or everyday items from Bible times. Examples of answers could be: the lost sheep, the coat of many colors, salt, the temple, the reed basket in which Moses was hidden, the cross, etc.

"Where Am I?"—Same procedure. Place names are used from the settings of Bible events, missionary journeys, modern missionary work, and so on. Examples might be: Red Sea, Sea of Galilee, Jerusalem, Bethlehem, Egypt, Mount Sinai, Golgotha, Garden of Gethsemane, and so forth.

Bulletin Boards

The following three pages feature bulletin boards which incorporate and display creative writing activities. Each set of instructions gives two or three ways each board can be used.

This Is Your Life!

Materials needed:

Background—blue bulletin board paper

Border—yellow or brown paper and aluminum foil. Paper should be 5½″ wide. At evenly spaced intervals, trace around a cup for cup-sized circles. Cut out circles. Tape aluminum foil to back over holes. Shiny side of foil should show on finished side of border.

Letters—yellow or brown to match border

Board #1—Student Recognition

Children write a one page autobiography of their lives, families, hobbies, school, pets, interests, etc. Younger children draw a picture and dictate a story to the teacher who writes it down for them.

Board #2—Bible Character Emphasis

Children write biography or short character sketches of Biblical personalities featured in unit or quarter lesson work. Teacher may add pictures of these Bible people from old materials or picture file.

Newspaper Reporting

Materials needed:

Background—old black and white newspapers

Letters—red paper (For lettering suggestions see "Title" sections below.)

Border—red paper strips, 2″ or 3″ wide

Student created newspaper accounts—printed or typed on white paper

Special instructions:

Students write news copy accounts of the material teacher is presenting. Board titles depend on material. Teacher may type stories before pinning them to board.

Board #1—Biblical News

Children write up information from lesson as if they were newspaper writers.

Title—Relate to location of stories such as: "Jerusalem News," "Bethlehem Gazette," "Corinthian Crier," or "Egyptian Enquirer."

Board #2—Local News

Children write news accounts of current events in local children's church activities. May include pictures.

Title—Use your own church name such as: "Trinity Chapel News" or "Stone Church Tablets."

Board #3—Mission News

Children write stories based on news which has or might occur on a mission field your church supports.

Title—Include location name such as: "The News of India" or "The African Express."

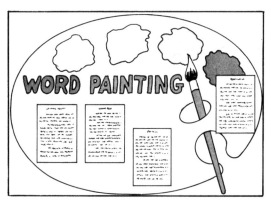

Word Painting

Materials needed:

Background—blue or white bulletin board paper

Palette—brown construction paper cut in oval shape

Paint splotches—brightly colored construction paper

Lettering—one of the paint splotch colors

Brush—black, grey, or brown paper *(or large kindergarten type paint brush, slant pinned to board)*

Special Instructions:

Explain to children how people can paint pictures by using descriptive words. Others can see the pictures in their minds. When children have completed writing efforts, display on board.

Board #1—Descriptions of Nature

Children write descriptions of natural items or scenes from God's world such as: a leaf, a flower, rainbow, scenic spot, etc.

Board #2—Biblical Descriptions

Children describe some place, event, or person from the Bible. Examples: Heaven, Jesus, Garden of Eden, etc.

MEMORY WORK

Those things learned well in childhood stay with us much more clearly than what we learn later in life. When children repeat God's word over and over for memorization, it becomes part of them even if they can't recall the exact wording later.

Memory work can be an exciting addition to Bible learning during Sunday school.

When planning memory work, it is necessary to make allowances for different abililty levels. Some children have difficulty learning even simplified verses. Older children are more aware and self-conscious about poor reading and memorizing skills. Modify and shorten the verse if necessary. Work with slower children in private if they are embarrassed to work in the group. Make every opportunity possible for each child to feel a sense of enjoyment and accomplishment in memorizing God's Word. Always include a few very easy verses so all children receive praise and special recognition.

Every time a child works with an adult or helper to say a memory verse, that adult has a chance to build the child's self-esteem, his feeling of welcome and belonging at Sunday school, his respect for Christians, and his knowledge of God's Word.

Charts

Educational supply shops and some variety stores carry poster-like charts for record keeping. The charts come in different colors, sizes, styles, and prices. Achievements may be recorded with marking pen, a variety of cute dots, or matching chart stickers.

Plan chart for units or quarters. Write item to be memorized on slanted line at chart top. Many charts have enough space for additional memorization projects—books of the Bible, disciple names, etc.

Booklets

The quarter's verses can be put in puzzle form. Staple the puzzles into booklets. Put a checklist in front part of book. *(See sample checklist in this section.)* Children work at learning verses each Sunday. Each completed verse is verified in the student's book by a sticker or an adult's initials.

Memory Training

A picture-memory program children enjoy is the Jerry Lucas memory training book, *Ready-Set-Believe.* Children can learn the books of the Bible, fruits of the Spirit, etc. Draw a mural to match the pictures. Children color during their spare time, and it reinforces visual imaging. *(Address for Jerry Lucas is Memory Training, P.O. Box 817, Fremont, CA 94537.)*

Bulletin Boards

One activity children really enjoy is the "Trading Post" or "Country Store." Use a bulletin board to illustrate the trading post or country store theme. This also displays the memory work chart, adds visual impact, and encourages students. *(See sample and instructions in this section.)*

At quarter's end, children trade accumulated dots for prizes. The more dots earned, the better the prize. Example: 1-5 dots = Scripture pencil and cute shaped eraser, 6-10 dots = Bible jigsaw puzzle, 11-15 dots = Bible story comic book, 16-20 dots = religious record. *(Prizes may be whatever is affordable and available.)*

There are many official looking award certificates and "Super Kid" type awards for recognition.

Combining charts on a bulletin board with student notebooks, provides a project for an entire quarter. Add extra credit verses or activities. Children are doing something fun and beneficial with spare moments and presession times that can be discipline hazards.

Country Store Bulletin Board

Materials needed:
Background—Nearly any color of paper, burlap, flannel, or old sheet
Canopy—One flat curtain rod or stick, nearly the width of the board
        One curtain rod which stands out two inches
        One striped or awning-like curtain valance

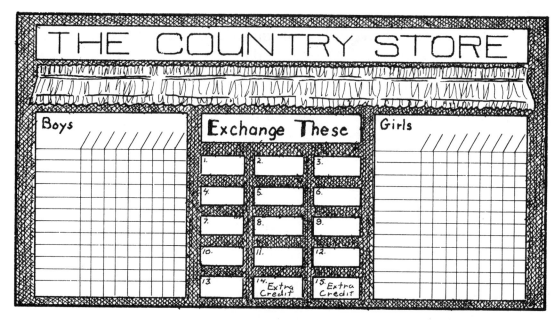

Store Sign—White butcher paper
Black felt-tip pen for lettering
Student Charts—Incentive charts, small size (14½″ x 21½″)
Bible Verse Cards—3″ x 5″ blank white index cards on which to print
Special instructions:

This board works for an entire quarter. Children memorize verses each week. They receive a small dot or smile face for each verse learned. At quarter's end, these dots are traded for prizes.

Valance may be attached to board with small nails, long tacks, or strong pins. *(See side view shown.)*

Trading Post Bulletin Board

Materials needed:

Background—Almost any solid color may be used. Tan burlap would be most in keeping with country or western theme. Bulletin board paper, flannel, cork, or old solid color sheets make backgrounds, too.

Sign Board—There are several ways this board can be made:

1. Use old board, as thin as possible, with letters burned into wood. Drill four small holes in corners. Attach to bulletin board with four small nails.

2. Use old board as above. Glue small rope or cord on for letters. Attach as in #1.

3. Use brown construction or bulletin board paper. Cut to look like board. Make letters with black felt-tip pen. Staple or pin to board.

Student Chart—Incentive chart, large size (21½″ x 28½″), may be bought in educational or church supply store, along with small colored dots or smiling face stickers to mark squares. Or they may be handmade from colored or butcher paper.

Trade-in Chart—Make chart same size as student chart. Type or print verses on blank white or colored 3″ x 5″ cards. Make chart title sign. Glue sign and cards. Rubber cement works best because it doesn't cause paper to warp, and excess glue can be rolled off.

Special instructions:

This bulletin board can be used for an entire quarter. *(See previous pages for instructions.)* The two charts may have small cord or rope between board and charts. This simulates the look of being attached to sign board.

Record Sheet

This sheet may be placed in front of puzzle and memorization booklet. Teacher or helper initials box when work is completed and when verse is memorized.

FOOD

Food appeals. Magazines, newspapers, radio and television commercials all reinforce the pleasure and satisfaction found in eating. Children enjoy eating. They will often work surprisingly hard for a tasty reward.

Educators know understanding and retention improve as more of the five basic senses are included in the learning process. Add taste, smell, and touch to sight and sound. A child will recall a lesson involving food much longer than a lecture-type lesson. Recall reinforces the personal application of Bible truth that teachers intend as a lesson result.

Ice cream cones, cookies, hamburgers, and treats add incentive when used as rewards for contests, memory work, or attendance.

Certain Sunday-school lessons gain impact and are naturals for including food. Object lessons increase in value. Even art is more fun when it can be eaten.

Learning, recall, art, enjoyment—all are underlined by the addition of food.

Bible Stories

The Fruits of the Spirit (Galatians 5:22, 23)

Cut some fresh fruit, bananas and apples, on Saturday to brown for a day. Arrange on a decorative plate Sunday morning with freshly cut fruit. Explain that you have a treat for each child. *(Have enough nice pieces of fruit for each child.)* After all have taken a fresh piece, ask why no one took the bad pieces. This is an excellent lead-in to how others feel about the good and bad qualitites in our lives.

The Feeding of the Five Thousand (John 6:1-15)

Bring to class five wheat rolls, two small smoked fish, or two pieces of smoked fish, and several small baskets. During the lesson, break the rolls and fish into little pieces. Pass baskets around the group so each child gets some.

The Barren Fig Tree (Luke 13:6-9) and *The Fig Tree* (Matthew 21:18-22)

Use dried figs or fig cookies to show the children what kind of fruit is being spoken of in these two stories.

Adam and Eve—the Temptation (Genesis 3)

Give an apple as a treat to each child. If children question the kind of fruit on the forbidden tree, explain that no one knows definitely. It was the act of disobedience rather than the type of fruit eaten which caused God's displeasure.

Jacob and Esau—the Birthright (Genesis 25)

During or after the lesson, each child could be given a small bowl of stew. The Bible calls the dish pottage. Pottage is a lentil soup. Perhaps it had meat in it, for Genesis calls it *red* pottage in verse 30. You may wish to make your own soup, or purchase a canned lentil soup.

Daniel and His Friends Make a Wise Choice (Daniel 1:3-20)

This lesson teaches of Daniel and his friends. They chose not to eat the king's rich food. Some of these foods were forbidden by Jewish law or avoided by Jewish custom. Serve fresh vegetables and ice water as a reminder of what these Jewish boys ate.

Queen Esther Prepares a Banquet (Esther 5:1-8; 7:1-10)

Use a small table. Cover the table with a tablecloth. Set the table as if for an elaborate meal. Use a few sweets, dessert, and goblets of red juice. Have two boys and a girl role play King Ahasuerus, Haman, and Esther. The Jews still celebrate this occasion with the feast called Purim.

Elijah and the Widow (1 Kings 17:8-16)

Oil and cornmeal may be used as illustrations of the oil and meal in the widow's cruse and barrel. Cornbread or cornmeal muffins give children an approximate taste of what the meal cakes might have been like.

Elijah, Elisha, and the Double Portion (2 Kings 2:6-15)

According to Jewish law (Deuteronomy 21:15-17), the firstborn son received a double portion of his father's wealth. Every other son received a single portion. Illustrate this by bringing six or seven boys to the front of the class. Each boy is given a single piece of some treat *(gum, gumdrops, etc.).* One child is told *he* is the oldest, and he receives an additional piece. Explain that Elisha asked for a double portion of Elijah's spiritual influence because he considered himself Elijah's firstborn spiritual son.

The Last Supper—Communion (Matthew 26:17-30)

Use grape juice and bits of flat crackers or bread. Teachers of younger children might just show the items and explain about them. Teachers with older children may plan an actual communion service with Scriptures, explanations, hymns, and prayer. Be certain the children understand the seriousness of the service. Offer a definite time to pray and ask forgiveness.

"I am the vine, ye are the branches" (John 15:1-8).

For this or any lesson that discusses vines and vineyards, grapes may be served.

Jesus—the Bread of Life (John 6:26-35)

For this or any lesson that discusses bread, small loaves or rolls may be used. Small loaves may be divided among the children.

Art

Church Window Cookies

Use this recipe, your own recipe, or a plain cookie mix.

1/3 cup shortening	2 3/4 cups all purpose flour
1/3 cup sugar	1 teaspoon soda
1 egg	1 teaspoon salt
2/3 cup honey	1 teaspoon vanilla

Mix shortening, sugar, egg, honey, and vanilla thoroughly. Sift together salt, soda, and flour. Mix well. Cover and chill dough. Bake at 375° for 8 to 10 minutes. Before baking:

1. Roll dough into strips about 1/4" thick. If dough becomes too sticky, rechill.
2. Make designs on aluminum foil. Be certain joinings are strong. Don't leave too wide an opening between design parts. Place foil on cookie sheet.
3. Crush lollipops. Sprinkle in openings.
4. Bake as directed above.

5. Cool. Peel off foil when cookie has hardened. *(Peel carefully.)*

All-Occasion Cutout Cookies

The cookie recipe already given works well for cutout cookies. Prepare dough ahead of time. Keep refrigerated until ready to roll. Flour surface of counter or board. Roll dough out to ¼″ thickness. Children cut cookies out with cookie cutter. Bake on lightly greased cookie sheet 8 to 10 minutes, or until no imprint remains when touched lightly. There are countless cookie cutters of plastic and metal to match any occasion.

Happy Face Cookies

Bake or buy sugar cookies. Purchase yellow frosting in decorator tube, or make your own. For very small children, make the happy face—two dot eyes and a curved line for a smile. Older children want to make their own happy face on the cookie.

Church Window Cookie

Happy Face Cookie

Butterfly Cookie

Cross Cake

Use a cake pan shaped like a cross if you have one. Teacher may frost or decorate cake for younger children. Give each one a piece on Easter Sunday. Older children enjoy doing part of the decorating. The teacher should prepare decorator frosting bags beforehand.

Bake cake in 9″ x 12″ x 2″ pan. Cut in the shape of a cross. Freeze. Make a thin frosting. Frost cut sides. Let frosting dry. Then frost or decorate the entire cake with normal frosting.

Dough Sculpture

Basic bread recipe:	3 tablespoons of sugar (honey)	1½ teaspoons salt
1 package yeast	¼ cup oil	
2 cups warm water	7 cups all purpose flour	

Put yeast in warm sugar water. Let stand five minutes to start yeast working. Add salt, oil, and flour a little at a time until you can work dough with hands. If sticky, add more flour. Knead.

Make dough sculpture on baking sheet or aluminum foil. Dough sculpture must lie flat, not standing. Make flat pancake shapes, rod shapes, and ball shapes. Stick them together with a little water. The parts will grow together as the dough rises. Let them rise 20 minutes. Bake at 350° 20 to 30 minutes. Time depends on size and thickness of figure.

Object Lessons

Saying Thank-You

The purpose of this object lesson is to show students how often we take the gifts and blessings of God for granted. We enjoy all the good things He has provided. We talk to Him, but we often forget to thank Him. Generally, we bring only our problems and complaints.

Place orange slices *(or some other treat)* on a plate. Say to the children, "We have a special treat for you today because we enjoy being with you on Sundays." Have the children walk by in single file to pick up a treat. Choose another adult to help you remember which children say thank-you.

After the treat is eaten, call to the front those children who said thank-you. Praise them. Then remind the children of how we accept all God's good gifts *(enumerate)* and forget to say thank-you.

Join hands in a circle. Have children each give a sentence prayer about one thing for which they are thankful.

"Giving thanks always for all things unto God and the Father in the name of our Lord Jesus Christ" (Ephesians 5:20).

Who Gets the Biggest Piece?

The purpose of this object lesson is to teach children that God's Word says we should share the biggest or best of what we have with others. We should not always try to keep the best for ourselves.

Bake and frost the necessary size sheet cake for your group. Serve cake on small paper plates. Mark an X in the center of one plate. That plate will hold the smallest piece. Cut the cake into nearly equal sized pieces, making certain that one piece is smaller. Put the smallest piece on the plate with the X, completely covering the X. Have a small, inexpensive gift wrapped.

Let the children come to the table where cake is. Let them choose their own piece. Tell them to save their plates when they are finished. When the cake is eaten, have the child with the X marked plate come to the front. Give him the gift and praise him for not taking the largest piece. Read Romans 12:10. Explain the verse and apply it to their lives.

"Be kindly affectioned one to another with brotherly love; in honor preferring one another" *(Romans 12:10).*

GAMES

Games are one of the Sunday-school teacher's best friends for many reasons. INVOLVEMENT: Games involve the children with each other so they become better acquainted and feel more a part of the group. REVIEW: Games are an excellent way to review Bible verses and Sunday-school lessons. Some children will learn verses for a game they wouldn't for regular classwork. More learning may take place during the game than during the lesson! PACE CHANGE: Games are a pace change from sitting and learning more passively during the lesson and table work. Games release that stored energy. ATMOSPHERE: Games create an atmosphere of enjoyment, especially important to children from nonchurch homes. They need to see that Christian living and learning can be fun.

Games need not be involved or expensive. There are some games on cards such as "Who Am I?," "What Am I?," and "Bible Authors." Every Bible supply store has some board games on heavy tagboard or cardboard. Individual moving pieces and spinners can be purchased at educational supply stores.

Time spent making reusable games saves valuable time later. Games made with plastic—if folded and stored carefully—can last for years. Games made from paper or tagboard can be laminated. Covered with clear contact paper, or slipped into thin plastic photo album pages. Most Sunday-school publishers repeat lesson materials every year to two years so the reusable games provide lesson enrichment over and over.

Occasionally a Sunday-school activity will take less time than expected, or someone will be unable to follow through with a planned activity. This is the perfect time to get a game from the permanent or reusable supplies. Games can save the Sunday-school teacher from loss of important Sunday-school learning time, and from discipline headaches created by too much free time.

Games are one of the teacher's best friends.

Bible Bingo

Equipment:
   Bingo pages
   Construction paper squares for markers
   Decorated coffee can with lid

Procedure:
1. Place a religious sticker in the free space on each bingo card. There is room on either side of the heading for additional stickers as decorations.
2. Bible characters, names of Old and New Testament books, verse references, etc., provide possible information for bingo squares. Fill in randomly.
3. Make a master copy. Put all pieces of information on separate squares of paper, place in coffee can, and shake. Draw one paper at a time from the can and call out for the children. Cover on the master copy so children's cards may be checked.
4. Bingo sheets made with sixteen or twenty squares work well for younger children, or when less information is desired on the card.

   Holiday Version:
      Children use candies for markers. When game is over, each child may eat his candy. Suggestions: February—candy hearts, April—jelly beans, October and November—candy corn, December—small red and green gumdrops.

Bible Bingo

B	I	N	G	O

Animal Pairs

Equipment:

Blindfolds for half the children

Chairs for half the group size

Procedure:

1. Ask children to match up in pairs.

2. Assign an animal name with an easily imitated noise to each pair of children.

3. Put chairs in a circle, facing inward, with several feet between each chair.

4. Explain that one of each pair of children is taken from the room, blindfolded, and led back into the room. The other half of each pair stands behind a chair, imitating the sound of the animal assigned to that pair.

5. Blindfolded child tries to find his partner and sit in the chair before any other child. His sole means of finding direction is the animal noise made by his partner.

6. Blindfold other half of group and repeat.

7. This game may be played in conjunction with any Bible lesson dealing with animals *(creation, Noah's ark, God's care for the world He created, etc.).*

Who Am I?

Equipment:

Style A • Masking tape, ball-point pen

Style B • Construction paper, pen, safety pin

Procedure:

Style A • Write the names of well-known Bible people on a long strip of masking tape. Prepare as many names as number of students usually in attendance. At game time, roll the tape back off the roll, cutting between each Bible name. Put one name on each child's forehead or back. Caution child to keep eyes closed while name is being attached.

Style B • Same procedure as in Style A except names are prepared on squares of construction paper and pinned to student's back.

1. Children try to discover the name of their Bible character by asking other children or adults questions about that Bible person. Questions must be ones answerable by "Yes" or "No." Child can ask no more than two questions of any person.

106

2. Have two teachers stage a sample demonstration showing children the kinds of questions to ask.

Bible Drills

1. Each child has a Bible.
2. Leader calls out a reference.
3. First child to stand and read the verse gets a point.
4. Class may play as individuals or as teams. In order to give all children a chance to play, it may be necessary to have a "Champion Club." Children who win three or four times for their team would have their names placed on the "Champion Club" list and be retired from that round or game.

Jigsaw Puzzles

Equipment:

Cardboard puzzles—inexpensive ten-twelve pieces

Procedure:

Game One • Each child has a puzzle. Children are timed. Puzzles are exchanged for second, third, or as many rounds as there is time to play.

Game Two • Divide children into small groups of not more than four. Each team works a puzzle. Game Two utilizes a few puzzles when there are not enough for each child.

Takeoffs From Childhood Games

Hot Potato

Equipment:

Clean potato

Bible verse

Procedure:

1. All children but one stand in a circle.
2. One child stands in the center of the circle holding the potato.
3. Child in center tosses the potato to one of the children in the circle. Child who catches potato must say the Bible verse. If he succeeds, he stays in the circle and tosses potato back to child in center.
4. If child who catches potato is unable to say verse, he changes places with child in center.
5. Move game quickly. If group is large, break into several smaller groups. In this way, more children get a turn and must say the verse.

Charades

Procedure:

1. Works best with children third grade or older. It can be played with younger children, but they need much coaching and story must be simple.
2. Divide class into as many groups as needed to be certain each child participates.
3. Children get together in a huddle to decide what recently learned Bible story they wish to act out. Even older children sometimes need guidance choosing a story or story portion.
4. When huddle or planning time is up, all children return to their seats for performances.
5. Each group takes a turn presenting its charade for other children to guess. Continue until all groups have had a chance to perform.

Human Tick-Tack-Toe

Equipment:

Style A • Black plastic playing surface

Style B • Masking tape or crepe paper strips

Game Setup:

Style A • Playing surface is made of a large sheet of thin, black plastic with wide masking tape lines. *(See example A.)* Plastic may be folded and stored.

Style B • Tape or paper strips are laid on floor to make tick-tack-toe diagram. *(See example B.)*

Style A   Style B

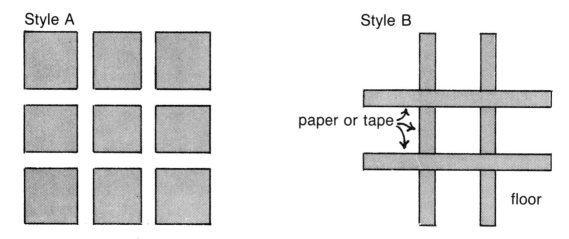

Procedure:

1. Have children divide into two teams. It is easier to tell teams apart if girls are on one team and boys on the other. If sex distribution is not even enough for equal teams, have children wear two different colored tags to represent X and O teams
2. Ask review questions in this way: If a team X member answers correctly, that member goes to stand in a tick-tack-toe square of his choice as a human marker. If a team X member misses, however, team O gets one

chance to answer that question. If they succeed, an O member fills a square. If O team member is unsuccessful, square stays empty. It is then team O's normal turn.

3. First team to get three in a row wins.

Blind Man's Guess

Equipment:
   Blindfold
Procedure:

1. Children hold hands to form a circle, then drop hands. Children must not move from the spot where they are standing when the game begins.

2. One child is placed in the center of the circle, blindfolded. He is spun around a few times. He then tries to catch someone in the circle.

3. Children in the circle may try to evade the blindfolded child by moving their upper body back and forth, but they must not move their feet.

4. When blindfolded child catches someone, he tries to guess the name of person caught. If he guesses correctly, the captured child must say the day's Bible verse. The captured child may stay in the outer circle if he can say the verse. If he can't, the blindfolded child says the verse and the two children exchange places. Captured child is blindfolded, turned around, and game goes on.

Hangman

Equipment:
   Chalk and blackboard
Procedure:

1. An adult draws the hangman's stand on board for each team.

2. Here is a sample board set up:

ABCDEFGHIJKLM

NOPQRSTUVWXYZ

ABCDEFGHIJKLM

NOPQRSTUVWXYZ

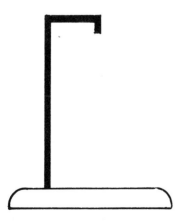

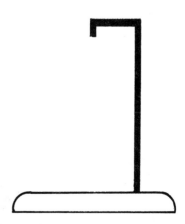

Team 1's word (angel)   Team 2's word (sheep)

3. Each team chooses a word having something to do with the day's lesson. It might be helpful to have some adult supervision in choosing the word.
4. To keep the game fair, the words chosen should not be more than two letters different in length. The game leader should announce before children choose words what word length will be. Say something like, "Choose a word with six or seven letters." Length of word depends partly on age and reading ability of children.
5. Adult supervising blackboard finds out each team's word. He then draws the correct number of blank spaces under each hangman stand.
6. Team One guesses a letter from Team Two's list. If they are correct, the letter is filled in on the appropriate blank or blanks in the word. If there are two or more of the same letter, all are filled in when the letter is called. As long as Team One calls letters correctly, they continue to play. When Team One misses a letter, the circle for the head is drawn on their hangman stand. Then Team Two takes a turn in the same manner.
7. As each letter is called, cross it from the list above the stand.
8. This game can be made to last a long time, depending on how detailed the stick figure is drawn. The head could consist of circle, eyes, nose, mouth, and ears before going on to the neck. The head could also have hair, eyebrows, etc.
9. Play continues until a team figures out the other team's word *(which makes them the winner)* or a team has hung themselves on the hangman's stand *(which makes them the loser)*.

Button, Button, Who's Got the Button?

Equipment:
  Button
  Bible verse
Procedure:
1. Works best with younger children. If verse is simple, even kindergarten children enjoy this.
2. All children but one sit in a circle on the floor. They sit close, cross-legged, knees nearly touching so it is easier to pass the button.
3. Children hold their hands in loose fists, palms down, fingers lightly curled inward. They move their hands back and forth to touch the hands of the people sitting on either side of them.
4. A button passes around the circle while all the children pretend to pass the button.
5. Child in center of the circle tries to catch someone passing the button. If he succeeds, the person caught with the button must say the Bible verse to stay in the circle on the floor. If he can't say the verse, he has to change places with the child in the center. Game continues in the same way.

110

Relay Races

Bible Verse Relay

Equipment:

   Yarn or tape to mark starting and turning places

Procedure:

1. Children form relay teams of equal size.
2. First child in each row races to the second string, says Bible verse to adult waiting there, and runs back. First team with all players finished wins.
3. An adult should supervise the starting line. Other adults need to be in place at second string turning place to hear student say Bible verse.

Bible Button-the-Shirt Relay

Equipment:

   Bible for each team

   Old, large man's shirt for each team

   Yarn or tape to mark starting place

Procedure:

1. Children form relay teams of equal size.
2. Each child must run to the place where shirt and Bible are for his team. He must put on and button up the shirt. Then he must look up whatever verse the teacher has assigned. Have adult standing by to help.
3. Child removes shirt and runs back to team.

Takeoffs From School

Bible Spelldown

Procedure:

1. Divide children into two teams.
2. Teams line up on opposite sides of the room.
3. Teacher alternates sides as he/she asks questions. Base questions on memory, lesson, or Bible information.
4. Team members who answer correctly remain standing.
5. Continue until one person is left. That team wins.
6. If time is limited, call as winner the team with most members standing.

Bible Match-up

Type A • Books of the Bible

Equipment:

   Flannel—to cover a bulletin board

   "Books of the Bible," Pict-O-Graph, #2265, Standard Publishing

Procedure:

Game One • Place flannel on bulletin board. Using flannelgraph pieces naming books of Bible, match book titles to headings of Old Testament or New Testament.

Game Two • Play with just Old Testament or New Testament set. Put up the categories for type of books. Children match individual books to the category into which they fall—such as Gospels, History, Epistles, Prophecy, etc.

Preserving materials:

Preparation—Lay the book pages from "Books of the Bible" face down on clear contact paper or clear book jacket paper. Press firmly with hands so page surface adheres well. Cut pieces apart and trim around edges.

Storage—Save book cover and inside information about other ways to use book. A blank page is provided which may be taped to back cover. Store individual pieces in this pocket. Keep book upright.

Type B • Verse Review

Equipment:

Construction paper, felt-tip pens

Procedure:

1. Write the beginning of several Bible verses on separate pieces of paper. Write verse endings on other pieces of paper. Mix. Distribute to children.

2. Children see how long it takes to match the verse beginnings and endings. Play as individuals or in teams. Teams may be timed to add excitement.

Sport Takeoffs

Bible Bowling

Equipment:

Bowling lane—a thin, black or clear plastic sheet 45-50" wide and 10' long

Bowling pins—white contact paper circles the size of a saucer. These are stuck on one end of the plastic lane, arranged, and numbered as shown in example.

Bowling ball—brightly colored bean bag

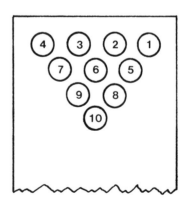

Procedure:

1. Place lane with circle end against a wall. Bean bag will not slide off end and child has better chance to score.

2. Divide children into two teams. Teams take turns.

3. Child bowls bean bag. Give younger children more than one chance if necessary.
4. Teacher asks review question. If child knows answer, the points he bowled are added to his team's score.
5. Team with most points wins.
   Storage:
   Fold so none of the white circles are creased. Store flat. This equipment should last for years.
   Baseball
   Equipment:
   Bases—heavy colored sailcloth or denim, approximately 12" x 15". Pad with a couple layers of old blanket or polyester fiber fill. Bases should have just enough body so they don't feel flat when stood upon.
   Blackboard, chalk
   Procedure:
1. The game is played with outs, scores, and innings—just as in a regular baseball game. An adult keeps score at the blackboard.
2. Place bases around the room equal distance from each other to form a diamond.
3. The review questions are used as a ball. The adult who asks questions stands in the center of the diamond as pitcher.
4. If child answers correctly, he scores a hit and moves to first base. If the child misses the question, he is out. Each person on the team who moves around the bases and reaches home plate scores a point.
5. After an equal number of innings, the team with the most points wins.
   This game can also be played on the blackboard. It seems much more vivid to the children, however, to play it with bases and move around the room.

TV Takeoffs

Bible Business
1. Children are given a Bible character's name.
2. Clues are given for that person's occupation.
3. Teams take turns guessing until one gets answer.
4. Leader may give as many clues as necessary.
5. Winner could be team with two out of three or three out of five wins.
6. If there is a tie, schedule a play-off for the following Sunday.
   Bible Bowl
1. Each side chooses four players to be their team.
2. Teams are seated in front of the class. Four chairs are on one side of a moderator's podium and four are on the other.
3. Teacher gives questions. Children indicate they can answer by standing up. First one up answers for his team.
4. Correct answer gets the team ten points and a chance to answer a two or three part conference question for twenty or thirty points. On conference

questions, team members get a chance to compare answers before the final answer is called for.

5. All questions have a time limit. A simple bell or whistle calls time. Don't allow too long for children to answer questions or the game lags.

6. Team with most points at end of game time wins.

Kid Kubes

1. Nine children from group become panel. Panel is arranged this way: three children sit cross-legged on the floor at the front of the room, three children sit behind them on chairs, three children stand behind the chairs.

2. Each of the nine panel members holds a double-sided 8″ x 10″ card. This card has a large X in one color on one side and a large O of a different color on the other.

3. The rest of the children are divided equally into two teams. One side is X team and the other is O team.

4. Moderator asks the team going first to choose a panelist. When team has chosen, moderator asks that panelist a Bible review or lesson review question. Panelist answers.

5. The team choosing decides together whether to agree or disagree with panelist's answer. If correct, panelist shows their symbol. If incorrect, play goes to opposing team.

6. Play alternates whether teams give correct answer or not.

7. Game is over when one team gets three symbols (X or O) in a row. A television version of human tick-tack-toe, if you like!

Name That Song

Equipment:

Record player, tape recorder, piano, voice, or some combination of these.

Songbooks, records, or tapes. Make songs a mixture of familiar children's songs, choruses sung in church, and a few well-known adult hymns.

Procedure:

1. Children are divided into three teams.

2. Play or sing the first measure or two of the song. Children should be given more if recognition isn't immediate.

3. First round identification value per song is five points. The first team to correctly identify each tune gets the points.

4. When five songs have been played and identified, round one ends.

Choose the two highest scoring teams for the second round.

5. In the second round, identification value per song is ten points. Five songs are given for identification.

6. Winner is team scoring highest number of points after the two rounds and total of ten songs.

Team Tangles

Game takes ten children—five on each team. If group is larger, have two games going in different parts of the room. Less than five can play on a team, or more than five. However, as team size increases, each child gets fewer turns and game drags.

Equipment:

Game questions and answers—prepared ahead of time. *(In Family Feud, 100 audience members are surveyed to get answer order and value. This information must be arbitrarily assigned in the Sunday-school version.)* Answer values should add up to 100 points for each round of questioning.

Answer cards—prepare answer and answer number value for posting on board when students get correct answer. *(See sample diagram.)*

Chalkboard—used for scoring, or entire game

Procedure—Play:

1. Step One—The first child on each team stands by the leader. Leader asks the first round question. *(Example—"Name one of the best known books of the Old Testament.")* Child who replies with the highest scoring correct answer wins for his team the option to continue to play. If his team chooses not to play, the opposing team plays.

   Step Two—Playing team takes turns guessing the remaining answers until all answers have been revealed or three strikes have occurred. Whenever a team member misses the question, he receives a strike. If three strikes occur before all answers are given, opposing team gets one chance to reply correctly and steal that round's points. If they cannot supply one correct answer, the other team gets the points they earned even though they could not complete the round.

2. Play then proceeds to the round two question and round three question in the same fashion.

   Procedure—Scoring:

1. For the first round, use six to eight questions. Total points *possible* for this round equal 100. Team only receives number of points earned with correct replies.

2. In second round, double value of scores. Use five to seven answers. Total point value equals 200.

3. Third round, triple value of scores. Use four answers. Total point value possible is 300.

4. First team to reach 300 points wins. Game ends even if the round isn't finished.

5. This game is an adaptation, so some rules are slightly different. There is no fast money round as at the end of the real "Family Feud."

Sample questions and answers:

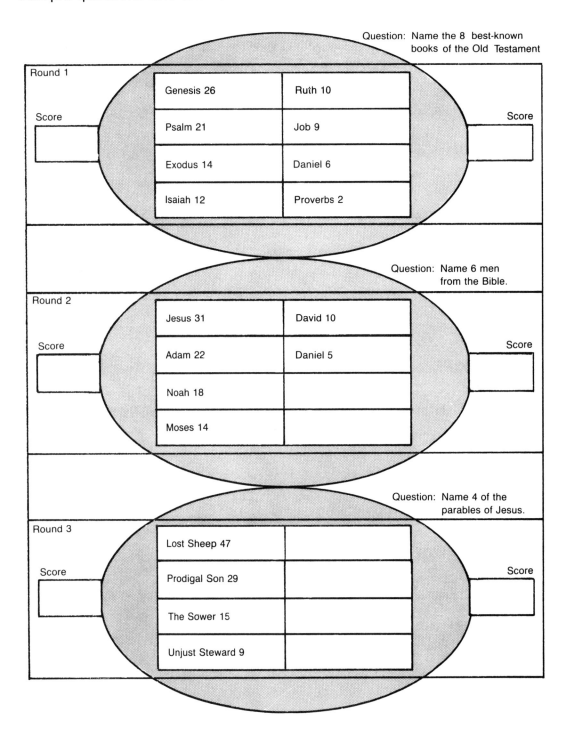

Question: Name the 8 best-known
books of the Old Testament

Round 1

Score

Genesis 26	Ruth 10
Psalm 21	Job 9
Exodus 14	Daniel 6
Isaiah 12	Proverbs 2

Score

Question: Name 6 men
from the Bible.

Round 2

Score

Jesus 31	David 10
Adam 22	Daniel 5
Noah 18	
Moses 14	

Score

Question: Name 4 of the
parables of Jesus.

Round 3

Score

Lost Sheep 47	
Prodigal Son 29	
The Sower 15	
Unjust Steward 9	

Score

Initial Blocks

Equipment:

Honeycomb grid *(Permission granted to copy grid.)*

Screen or blank wall

Washable overhead transparency pens—black, red, and blue

Procedure:

1. Choose twenty Bible people, places, animals, things, books of the Bible, etc., or combination, to fit lesson or quarter.
   a. Make twenty questions—one for each person, etc.
   b. Put first initial from each of the twenty answers in the cubes, one to each cube until all cubes and all answers are used. Use black pen.
   c. If three or four names begin with the same letter, the question will make clear what the answer should be *(Jesus, Joseph, Judas, James)*.
   d. Place transparency, ready for game, on overhead.
2. Divide group into thirds. Put two-thirds on Red team and one-third on Blue team. Appoint a captain for each team.
   a. Red team must go *across* the honeycomb in a zigzag line of touching hexagons. They must have a minimum of five hexagons touching across to win.
   b. Blue team goes from *top to bottom* or vice versa. They need four or more hexagons touching to win.
3. Teams alternate turns. When they answer correctly, color the hexagon their color. If they miss, however, the opposing team gets a chance to answer that question. If the opposition answers correctly, their color is placed in the hexagon, making a block. This chance to place a block is *not* the opposition team's normal turn.
   a. Red begins play. Group decides which hexagon, and captain calls it out. Question is given. Group decides answer, and captain calls it out. If correct, color hexagon Red. If not, Blue tries to block. Then Blue plays its normal turn.
   b. First team to get across grid in their direction wins.

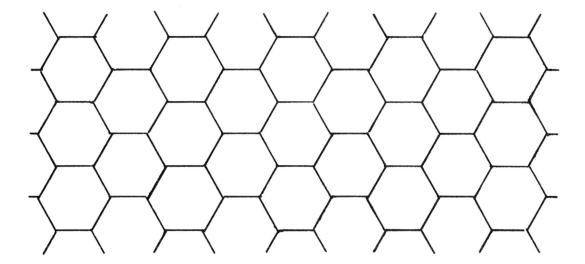

RESEARCH

Even younger children can learn from some research techniques. What we see and discover for ourselves usually has more lasting meaning than something we are told by someone else.

Use research as a separate activity preceding or following the lesson. Incorporate it into the lesson. Make it a separate occasion—such as a field trip—which provides information to be shared at the next group meeting.

Research may include such activities and materials as:

Field trips
Picture study
Bible dictionaries
Bible encyclopedias
Bible study books
Other Christian printed literature
Films
Filmstrips
Slides
Maps
Time lines
Bible study teams
Reading the Bible

Field Trips

Trips may be planned to correlate with a project in the department *(such as trip to radio or television studio)* or for information about God's world, how people live and worship, or to show children how people in need are cared for.

Preplanning

1. Decide what learning experience to provide for children.
2. Get permission for trip from pastor or department leader.
3. Check for parent support. Additional adults may be needed to drive or chaperone.
4. Call ahead to learn procedure for making trips to the establishment in mind. Set up an appointment time. *(Leader may wish to visit ahead of time to be truly prepared.)*
5. Arrange for bus driver if church transportation is to be used.
6. Arrange for adult drivers if personal cars are to be driven.
7. Get permission slips signed by parents for each child. *(See sample slip in this section.)*
8. Make informational handouts for place, date, time of departure, and return. Send these home with children at least two weeks before the proposed outing. Permission slip may be attached to bottom of handout.
9. Plan for one adult to accompany each five children.
10. To get maximum benefit from the trip, prepare a list of things for which you wish children to watch.
11. Have definite rules for behavior. Discuss with children before leaving appropriate behavior for field trips and especially for the place being visited.

Trip Follow-up

1. Discuss field trip.
2. Write thank you letters to adults who helped with trip, bus driver, and especially establishment visited.
3. Children may review learning by:
   a. Drawing pictures of what they saw.
   b. Making a bulletin board from pictures or informational pamphlets or pictures obtained during the trip.
   c. Writing reports about the trip.
   d. Making a bulletin board from reports written about trip.
   e. Making a bulletin board from pictures taken of children while on trip.
   f. Planning projects relating to field trip such as:
      -Making radio or television program.
      -Drawing sequence strip for TV box. *(See section on Art.)*
      -Making cards for people in nursing home.
      -Baking cookies or making craft items to give to people in nursing home.
   g. Sharing field trip experience, reports, or items brought back from trip with another department.

```
┌─────────────────────────────────────────────────────────────┐
│                                                               │
│                  FIELD TRIP INFORMATION                       │
│   To: Memorial Hospital, McDonalds                            │
│   Date: March 16th                                            │
│   Leave Church: 1:00 P.M.    Return: 3:30 P.M.                │
│   Transportation: Private cars                                │
│                          Detach here and return by March 15th.│
│   ----------------------------------------------------------- │
│       I give permission for my child, _____ ,  │
│   to attend the field trip to Memorial Hospital and McDonalds │
│   on March 16th.                                              │
│       I hereby release the (specific church name should be    │
│   inserted here) and individual drivers from liability in     │
│   case of injury.                                             │
│   Signed _____ Date _____    │
│                                                               │
└─────────────────────────────────────────────────────────────┘
```

Field Trip Suggestions

Nursing Home

Plan as a public service project. Many churches have older members living in nursing homes. Choose a home where residents are in fairly good health. If possible, go to one where some church members live. Children may come prepared to sing, share cards, cookies, or craft items they have made.

Hospital

Children learn about care given when people are ill or have emergencies. We teach them to trust in God for help and healing. Children may feel even more secure when they learn how much man can do to help others with the wisdom God has given.

Mission

Your community may have a mission. Children can learn what the church or religious community has to offer those whose lives are broken and in need of spiritual, physical, emotional, and financial help.

As a follow-up project, children can help gather food, clothing, or other items needed for the mission work.

Christian Bookstore

There is a tremendous variety of Christian literature available today, much of it for or related to children. Arrange to have a demonstration on how to choose a Bible and how to play a good record. Books for the age level of your group may be introduced to the children. If time allows, review a book or two.

Radio, Television Station

If possible in your community, arrange to visit a Christian owned or operated station. If planned adequately in advance, children may be able to watch the production of a program, or take part in some way.

Regular station operation, planning, and production may be set into a Christian context in the classroom. Techniques and procedures learned on the trip may be incorporated into planning done by class for their own production. *(See Drama section.)*

Museums

Local museum exhibits of artifacts from other cultures might build a better understanding of missionary work.

If Bible time exhibits are available, children will grow in understanding of life in the various times that famous Bible characters lived.

Industry, Craft

Seeing the complexity in production of items we often take for granted may increase children's awe of God and His creation. The more children realize the thought and planning necessary to make everyday things, the less they will believe the evolutionary theory that life and our earth were accidents. Teacher direction is needed to fully insure the children understand the comparison.

Libraries

Public and private libraries have many books pertaining to Bible times, culture, study, maps, people, history, etc.

Libraries also carry many books relating to craft, art, or other information children may need to plan projects for Sunday school.

Children's sections sometimes have specific books relating to games in Bible times, stitchery for Bible stories, etc.

Planetariums, Science Museums

Children learn a great deal about the world God created through these trips. Any conflicts in theoretical views regarding the origin of the earth may be dealt with back in the classroom.

Nature Hikes

These provide firsthand discovery of God's creation.

Nature walks may be done in local parks, around the church property for very small children, as part of day camp or backyard vacation Bible schools, during camp outs, or while at children's camps in the mountains or at the beach.

Permissible items brought back make good material for a display or bulletin board.

Farms, Ranches, Dairies

These trips provide yet another way to view part of God's creation. Children enjoy animals. Try to plan the trip in the spring when young animals may be seen or carefully handled.

Picture Study

Use picture study to gather information, compare past and present, contrast life-styles, or for other information. Pictures often show how people dressed, worked, ate, traveled, and worshiped. Pictures can represent Bible times, missionary or foreign work, and present-day activities.

Provide students with a list of things for which to look as they study the pictures. Discussion of study results may be oral with younger children.

Hymn Study

Much has gone into the making of our hymns in terms of Scripture, human interest—triumph over difficult circumstances, history, use, and music type. We take much of our music for granted. Children from fifth grade up may enjoy a unit of hymn study as an extra activity. They will sing and listen with greater appreciation as a result. Tapes and records chosen by the teacher are played to give examples of various kinds of religious music.

Studying song lyrics also gives much information. Care must be taken when using some contemporary music, however. Some of the lyrics are not truly accurate representations of Bible truth.

Worksheets

Study will be more effective if students record their newly gained information on a worksheet. Sheets may be stapled together in booklet form.

The teacher should do some advance review so songs chosen for student study are a variety of types. The song composers should have something interesting, inspiring, or unusual in their personal background.

A sample worksheet follows. Permission is granted to reproduce worksheet.

Hymn Study

Hymn Title _____

Composer _____

Lyricist *(if different from composer)* _____

_____

Type of Music:

Scripture	Contemporary	Chant
Classical	Folk/Ballad	Rock
Gospel	Country/Western	Other

Hymn History—What country composed in? Anything unusual about how or why the song was written?

_____
_____

Composer History—When lived, country, anything of interest about composer's life?

_____
_____

Lyricist History—When lived, country, anything of interest about lyricist's life?

_____
_____
_____

Bible Dictionaries, Bible Encyclopedias

Older children will be able to use Bible reference books to look up word meanings, uses of special objects and tools, research customs—both social and religious—animals, plants, clothing, and many other things.

Bible Study Books, Other Christian Printed Literature

Bible study books may be used for reference books. Even adult Bible study books, in modified form, have portions usable for older children.

Other printed literature may include story papers, old take-home booklets, some selected material from publishers other than your own, old hymnbooks, or suitable materials at the local Christian bookstore.

Films, Filmstrips, Slides, Records, Cassettes

Films, filmstrips, and slides furnish information for research in much the same way as pictures. Records and cassettes may be used as a tool for studying lyrics or as a listening activity. *(See Hymn Study.)*

Maps, Charts, Time Lines

Many Bibles have map sections in the back. These give some basic information about places and boundaries of different Bible times.

There are good books with many maps and pictures for Bible study. Your local Christian bookstore carries or can order these for you.

Reader's Digest has a beautiful book of maps and pictures of the Holy Land. It may be borrowed from the public library, along with other oversize books relating to the Holy Land.

A Bible time line shows a section of Bible history in chronological order. Events are written on perpendicular or slanted lines along a straight line.

| 1000 BC | David | Solomon | Kingdom divided | 900 BC | Elijah | 800 BC | Jonah | 700 BC | Jeremiah | 600 BC | Daniel | Ezekiel | 500 BC | Ezra |

Many children have no firm idea of the sequence of Bible happenings. They have been taught many Bible stories in segments unrelated to the progression of historical events. A time line helps children pull together much fragmented information.

Bible Study Teams

Divide children into small groups. Give each group a particular aspect of a topic or a separate topic related to a general theme. Teams are given a set of Bible references. *(These may be coordinated from a Bible concordance.)* Team members look up verses, record information, and share when group discusses study results.

Children will remember much longer what they discover for themselves with their friends. Older children want to work independently. Adult supervision is necessary to set up teams and to draw together all the pieces of information gathered by students.

ORAL
COMMUNICATION

Conversation is one of the main feedback tools teachers have to gage the extent of learning and understanding from a Sunday-school presentation.

Group communication should have an open, friendly atmosphere. Children should be encouraged to participate in discussion. Teachers can do this by maintaining eye contact, smiling, and calling on children. Some children feel intimidated by larger groups, so work in small groups occasionally for Bible application discussions. When guiding discussions, use questions that ask "Why?" or "How would you feel?" or "What would you do?" to stimulate real thinking rather than giving questions that just have "Yes" or "No" answers. Be listening during conversational activities for misconceptions. The confused areas can be explained or retaught if necessary.

There are many oral communication techniques available for enriching presentation of Bible truths. These actively involve the child, which greatly increases his learning. The most common oral communication techniques are:

Sharing   Storytelling
Discussion   Buzz Groups
Listening Teams   Conversation
Interviews   Choral Speaking
Brainstorming   Bible Reading

Sharing

To share means to have an equal part or portion. Sharing verbally means each person gets an opportunity to participate. Teachers need to guard each child's equal sharing opportunity. As with adults, there are those children who are naturally verbal, those who are somewhat aggressive in speaking up, those who are shy or less confident. They need encouragement and prompting to participate.

Sharing may be of experiences, thoughts, feelings, ideas, or any topics of interest and value to the group.

Discussion

The word "discuss" is defined as an investigation of that which is uncertain, or an argument presenting various sides for the sake of arriving at truth.

Group Discussion

A discussion, then, in Sunday school should present various aspects of a subject. It doesn't mean random visiting. The teacher may want to look at several points of the topic and have some leading questions ready. She should have Scripture references ready so children can look up information from the Bible. This technique is good for teaching children that God's Word is the final authority.

Speaker Discussion

If more than one speaker is present, varying points of view may be taken and discussed before the children.

One speaker could lead the discussion, or bounce ideas or opinions back and forth with the Sunday-school teachers or students.

Panel Discussion

In this type of discussion, two to five people share their ideas, knowledge, or experience on some general subject to which they can all relate. Panels may be adults from the church or other churches. They may be pastors, lay people, or children. One person generally acts as moderator to field questions and keep discussion evenly distributed among panel members, and on topic. If adults are to be invited as panel members, they should be aware of the general topic to be discussed. If each panel member is to emphasize a particular segment of a subject, they must know in advance in order to prepare.

Panels composed of children are one way to report on research projects or field trips.

Buzz Groups

This term is just another name for small discussion groups. The term comes from the sound of many voices buzzing during such an activity.

Buzz groups are small groups. Each group has a topic to discuss or questions to answer. Results are given during a group discussion or a group session led by the teacher.

Brainstorming

To brainstorm is to toss out ideas in a group situation. Each person contributes ideas. Ideas are sifted through, and the best ones chosen to proceed upon. This may be done for projects, puppet plays, drama, field trip suggestions, and so forth. It is good if children can have some input in decisions. Older children often have some very good thoughts—both related to possible projects or in response to lesson truths being translated into action or Christian behavior.

Choral Speaking

Bible verses, responsive readings, song lyrics spoken instead of sung, poetry, or drama are appropriate for choral speaking.

Small groups speak in unison in a variety of patterns. Boys may speak alternating verses. Girls form the other group. Both may join together for certain parts. Three parts may be used by having adult voices form one portion.

Location of voices may alter. Each group can be placed in a different part of the room as they speak.

Verses can be read directly from the Bible with older children. Younger children may need modified verses printed on newsprint or white butcher paper, hung in a central location so all can see. Very young children like repeating a particular phrase in certain parts as teacher leads "speaking." They also enjoy repeating a line from a story in the same way. Some children's stories repeat a phrase several times. A teacher can pick up on this and have the children say it with her each time.

Some suggested verses or chapters for choral speaking:

1. The Lord's Prayer (Matthew 6:9-15)
2. The Ten Commandments (Exodus 20:3-17)
3. The Beatitudes (Matthew 5:3-12)
4. The Love Chapter (1 Corinthians 13)
5. The Twenty-third Psalm
6. The Godly Man (Psalm 1)
7. Hymn of Praise (Psalm 100)
8. Hymn of Praise (Psalm 150)
9. Armor of God (Ephesians 6:10-18)

These chapters are longer and more appropriate for older children. If segments were used, younger children could enjoy these also.

1. Hymn of Salvation or Deliverance (Psalm 18)
2. Hymn of Hope and Trust (Psalm 37)
3. Hymn of Loving-Kindness of God (Psalm 138)
4. In Praise of God's Wonderful Creation (Psalm 104)
5. All Creation Praises God (Psalm 148)

Interviews

Interviews could begin in the Sunday-school department itself. Children may attend Sunday after Sunday without ever really getting to know their teachers. Department heads, teachers, pastors may be interviewed.

Interview children, also. Unless from small towns, many children attend different schools, have different friends, skills, interests, pets, and so on. Interviews help children get to know each other better. They make the child being interviewed feel important and special.

When doing interviews of adults, children should submit questions to the teacher a week before. These are given to the person being interviewed. In this way, the adult has some answers ready and will feel more confident about the interview. Teacher may need to guide the children in formation of questions and may need to add some of his/her own.

Besides getting better acquainted, interviews may show how others became Christians and how the Lord has helped them in their lives. We want our lives to be examples to those we teach. But many of our students know little of our lives or how the Lord has guided and helped us. Some of our students need the encouragement of knowing that some adult Christians came from divorced, non-Christian homes, or overcame great obstacles with God's unfailing support.

Some questions to ask an adult being interviewed:
1. Where did you live as a child?
2. Did you have brothers and sisters? How many?
3. What made you happy? What made you sad?
4. What kind of things did you like to do?
5. When did you find out about the Lord, or become a Christian?
6. What kind of work do you do now?
7. How did you come to be doing that work?
8. Does God help you in your daily living? How?
9. How has Bible reading and prayer changed or improved your life?

Children may be asked similar questions—with more emphasis on their daily lives, school, likes, dislikes, skills, family, etc.

Bible Reading

Bible reading for the Sunday-school class can be done by either the teacher or the children. If children are to read the Bible passage, you may wish to take them to one side and go over the Scripture beforehand. Children in second and third grade can read selected passages with some help on harder words.

When the child is reading before the group, the pre-reading and preparation will make the experience enjoyable for him.

Our children need the experience of being in front of others. Bible reading is an excellent opportunity to give children this practice, and it makes them feel necessary and important.

Listening Teams

Listening teams may be small *(2-4 people)* groups made up to listen with a specific purpose.

Teams may be used to listen to:

1. A pastor's sermon.
2. A special speaker's sermon.
3. A special singing group.
4. A particular type of music for hymn study.
5. Some civic activity that may have relevance to the church or some Bible topic.
6. Another church's service.
7. Experiences of older Christians.

All information gathered is brought back to the original class group. There it is sorted through—usually in a conversational way. Teacher helps pull out facts, ideas, and experiences she wants to use to reinforce or extend Bible truths being emphasized or taught.

Storytelling

Jesus was a great storyteller. His stories related directly to the everyday lives of people listening.

Prepare

Read the story quickly a few days to a week before teaching it. Let story events and meaning become very familiar. Pray as you study.

Final Study

Decide what is the most important point of the story. Write it down. Go over the events in the story, putting them in order, and decide the climax.

Telling the Story

1. Imagine yourself there in the story. Imagine the facial expressions of the people, the scene, the sounds, and the incidents.
2. Make the story vivid. When you can visualize the story and feel part of it, your listeners will, too. Make the people in the story seem alive, as if you could meet them on the street near your home.
3. Use words appropriate to age level so children will understand.
4. If story has several characters, use a different tone of voice for each one.
5. Sit near younger children, for they like to be near the person telling the story. Older children enjoy some movement and a little more variety.

Real-life Application

Use examples that will be relevant to the daily lives of the child you are teaching. Think about the most important concerns at this age. Try to remember what you enjoyed at that age, what frightened, excited, impressed, or helped you. Think of how you felt about friends, relatives, and pets. This will help you get on track for the feeling level of the child.